Born to Grieve

Born to Grieve

The Struggle to Survive

C. K. VETSCH

ARCHWAY
PUBLISHING

Archway Publishing books may be ordered
through booksellers or by contacting:

Archway Publishing
1663 Liberty Drive
Bloomington, IN 47403
www.archwaypublishing.com
1 (888) 242-5904

Because of the dynamic nature of the Internet, any web
addresses or links contained in this book may have changed
since publication and may no longer be valid. The views
expressed in this work are solely those of the author and do
not necessarily reflect the views of the publisher, and the
publisher hereby disclaims any responsibility for them.

Any people depicted in stock imagery provided
by Thinkstock are models, and such images are
being used for illustrative purposes only.
Certain stock imagery © Thinkstock.

ISBN: 978-1-4808-4869-6 (sc)
ISBN: 978-1-4808-4870-2 (e)

Library of Congress Control Number: 2017945928

Print information available on the last page.

Archway Publishing rev. date: 08/22/2017

Contents

This book is dedicated to Andie. She has the courage and commitment to quality of life to the highest degree I have ever experienced. When she was born, she had a fractured skull and quit breathing. After they resuscitated her, they did surgery to repair her skull. She was left with numerous disabilities. She has survived many years of insults and abuse common to those with severe disabilities. She has accomplished extraordinary things and is presently studying mathematics at a top university. She edited the final copy of this book. Thank you, Andie.

Introduction

In the process of writing this book, I was challenged by numerous individuals about the concept of being born to grieve. Most of those people could not comprehend how any person could actually be brought into this world with predestination to grieve. It seemed too ridiculous to believe that an unborn child or a newborn baby could be set up to grieve and carry that burden throughout a lifetime.

The stories of those children in this book will help explain how this can happen. Some were born with the burden of grief already waiting for them. Some children picked up that burden as older children carried it for life. Only those who have received the help they needed to recover have been able to set that burden down and live lives of fulfillment.

Read this book with an open mind. You may recognize the significance of this concept in your own life or in the life of someone else. If you are one of those children who were born to grieve, it is time for you to put down your burden. It is time for you to find wholeness in body, mind, and spirit.

It is also time to stop the cycle of this destructive

grief and prevent passing it down to the next generation and the next and so on. That is what happened in my family for more than one hundred and fifty years—and probably before that.

It is easier to build strong children than to repair broken men.

Frederick Douglass

Abandoned at Conception

The Unwanted Child

There are many reasons parents abuse their children. One of the most damaging is when a child was simply not wanted from the moment of conception. For some children, the abuse begins while they are still in the womb. From the moment the parents verify the pregnancy, that child begins a life of feeling unwanted, unloved, and burdensome to everyone. He or she is, in essence, programmed for abuse and grief from the moment of conception.

Consequently, some children never learn to trust or bond. They never experience what it feels like to be loved, and they may not have any opportunities to show love. They may become enmeshed in their parents' problems and may be given the total burden of responsibility for the success or failure of the family. Children take this responsibility seriously and believe the negative messages about them. No matter how hard they try, nothing they do is good enough. They have been brainwashed to believe they are a burden and are in a no-win situation.

Unfortunately, these children have nothing to build on. A child's self-confidence and self-esteem grows with each positive event in life. These children have done only unacceptable things and received only negative feedback from their parents. They have been made to believe that their births were mistakes and they are burdens. How can they ever feel good about themselves when they have never experienced positive stroking from their parents?

This bad nurturing may become even more destructive if the family has other problems such as alcoholism, financial distress, unemployment, loss of a significant person, serious illness, or divorce. The unwanted child may become an even greater target of abuse by parents or "wanted" siblings. To add to their distress, they will probably take responsibility for the family's unhappiness.

To add to the confusion, as unwanted children grow older, they may start to question some of the labels that have been attached to them. On the one hand, they feel that it is not true, they are not that way, and it just does not fit. If children have been exposed to one or two people, such as teachers, who give them a feeling of self-worth, they may become very distressed by the contradiction they sense. On one hand, they feel good about the positive feedback, but on the other hand, they doubt its sincerity. It must be because the person giving the positive feedback does not really know the child like his or her parents do. As children's minds say one thing, the voices of their parents' lifetime of imprinting grows louder.

Children may dutifully return to beliefs the parents have about them because otherwise they would betray their parents. They do not have enough self-confidence to believe they can become anything other than what their parents predicted. Due to fear of disagreeing with their parents, they are not willing to take risks in order to be themselves.

Another difficulty of these children is that even when they build up enough courage to have a positive belief about themselves or try a different behavior, they are bombarded with guilt. They feel as if they are betraying their parents by trying to be different from the way their parents see them. After all, who knows them better than their parents? When changes become visible to the parents, they may become critical and continue the pressure until they conform to the parents' expectations. The children are also terrified of failure each time they think about or try acting in a way that is different from what their parents have dictated. These children are in a no-win situation, and it may become easier to conform to the old ways than to risk rejection with new ways.

Here is one scenario: A girl has been taught to believe that her parents are always right. She has also convinced herself that the only way she can keep her parents happy is to agree with whatever they say. She will not risk their anger or rejection by believing differently about herself than her parents. She may strive even harder to fit into the mold her parents have made for her. She may do this even though she perceives herself in a different light than her parents see her. She has become a victim of mind battering by her parents and has never developed the skills to move beyond that victim role. She may be convinced that if her own parents do not love her, no one else could possibly love her. This becomes her justification for invalidating any positive reinforcement others try to give her. She does not trust their judgment or their motives. These parents usually impose this feeling of being worthless as a lifelong sentence so the child is left without even a hope for change in the future. She will carry the parents' immovable image of herself into adulthood unless she has counseling to believe otherwise. She may also become a mind-battering parent herself.

My mother was definitely abandoned at conception. Her mind battering was so complete that even after all her abusers died, she was still controlled by their injunctions from the grave. At the time of her death, she was still being controlled by the mind battering of her caregivers. She had suffered her entire life from the negative imprinting that started in the womb. Her mind was constantly replaying the terrible words and actions of the adults who abused her during childhood. She never believed they were wrong. She only believed that she was worthless and unlovable, and she blamed herself for all the pain in her life. What a terrible way to live for seventy-five years.

Another unfortunate outcome of mind battering is the way it affects a child's ability to learn. A child may be so preoccupied with the impact of the cruelty in his or her life that he cannot concentrate in school. Although the parents criticize him if he does not get good grades, they do not work with him at home or even praise them when he do well. The child may come home with four As and two A minuses on his report cards, but instead of receiving praise for high marks, he will be criticized for not getting all As.

I remember when I was in high school, and a guidance counselor suggested that I take typing. I went home very excited and told my mother I wanted to take typing. She looked at me sternly and said, "You can't learn to type because you can't play the piano." I never questioned her reasoning. I simply believed she knew the truth about everything, and so I did not take typing in high school. Several years later, after I left school and home, I asked myself what one had to do with the other. My conclusion was that the reason I could not play piano was because I could not read music and because I hated the required music in school. I never wanted to play piano! I signed up for a typing class and eventually learned to type at 130 words per minute. I have used my typing skills since then and still cannot play the piano.

It takes a great deal of courage to move away from parental injunctions that we have heard all of our life. Unfortunately, it also takes a lot of confidence to accept that we can actually do something and be someone contrary to what our parents have told us. Children who were abandoned at conception usually do not acquire the self-confidence to believe in themselves. Their self-esteem may be minimal, and they have few successful experiences to build on. Their primary role models are the parents who are guilty of mind battering.

Unfortunately, parent pleasing often continues into adulthood and causes them to remain wounded children. This will affect all of their relationships as adults and cause a great deal of conflict. It will also influence the way they treat their spouses and children. For example, a man may become very successful in the eyes of everyone around him and still only perceive himself as less-than-good-enough. The invisible scars from childhood will continue to fester unless he gets in-depth counseling to help him change the life script he was given in the womb by his parents.

My conception was definitely a mistake, and my parents constantly reminded me of that all of my life, especially my father. He tried to correct that mistake by having me aborted but failed to do so. In spite of all the truly marvelous things I have accomplished throughout my life, I never appreciated them as successes or real accomplishments because they were never quite good enough to be recognized as such by my parents. I always felt like they never forgave me for living when they tried to have me aborted.

My mother told me that she sold her breast milk to the county hospital after I was born because they paid high prices for breast milk to give to premature babies. That seemed like an even greater put-down than all the remarks about not having the courtesy to die! I waited for fifty years for her to put her arms around me and say, "I love you. I'm so proud of you, and I'm so glad that you are my daughter!" It never happened because she died and left me with a hole in my soul that could only be healed by healing the wounded child who had clung to that hope for love and acceptance for so many years. And yet I know that I am very fortunate because I have experienced the healing of my childhood wounds. My mother came into the world as a wounded child and left this world as a wounded child—without ever having received the love she so desperately needed.

I would not recommend carrying a wounded child for so many years, but it is better to have it healed at any age rather than to carry it to the grave with us as my mother did.

Born the Wrong Sex

A Terrible Discrimination

One of the saddest forms of discrimination is that which is brought against children simply because they were born the wrong sex. One or both parents may have wanted a child of a particular sex. Quite often, a son is preferred—and when a girl is born, the disappointment may set that child up to be ignored or abused.

If the sex of the baby is discovered early in the pregnancy and it is not the desired sex, some parents will attempt to have the baby aborted. Some mothers are so disappointed when they learn the child is not the desired sex, ad it adversely affects the remainder of the pregnancy. Some mothers become so depressed that the days are difficult to bear. Her depression in turn adversely affects her unborn child and can give the child a feeling of being unwanted and unloved. The child may then be born depressed and become difficult to soothe. The more difficult the child is to deal with, the more upset the mother becomes. That is the beginning of a very stressful relationship. The bonding that would normally take place between a mother and child who was truly wanted will not occur, making the situation even more intolerable.

A woman I know said, "This is really a wasted pregnancy. We wanted a boy. I wish we could just abort it and try again for a boy." They tried to have the baby aborted, but the doctor refused. She always referred to the baby as *it*—not her. It was as if the little girl had lost her identity and value even before she was born.

How significantly a child is affected by this discrimination depends a great deal on birth order and number of siblings. When I was born, boys were considered more valuable. Girls were considered necessary in order to produce more boys, to care for husbands, take care of households, and nothing more. It was considered important and necessary to educate boys beyond high school. As my father put it, "Girls don't need an education to change diapers and have sex." This attitude is still very prevalent today.

If a son is desired and born first, a daughter's birth may be anticlimactic. She may become a victim of neglect or abuse. The parents may have pinned all their hopes, dreams, and expectations on their son. They will even go so far as to pay special attention to his achievements, brag about him constantly to family and friends, celebrate his special days, and generally put him on a pedestal. He is everything they ever wanted and expected. Their joy and pride seems to bubble out all over.

An alienated father may ignore the child or abuse her emotionally and psychologically. In that case, the child will be unable to find nurturing in either parent. These considerations will affect the degree of neglect or abuse—and the extent of the damage. The damage might be permanent, depending upon the child's ability to live beyond the discrimination and find meaning despite their parent's terrible legacy of discrimination.

Unloved and Unwanted

My Mother's Story

I think the most tragic thing about my mother's life was that happiness eluded her most of her life. Over the years, she tried to end her life in multiple ways. She truly believed she was a terrible person who should have never been born.

She was the eighth child in her family. Her mother died when she was two years old as the result of a failed abortion. Her father decided that she would only be a burden on the farm and gave her to a Catholic orphanage. Her married, eighteen-year-old sister removed her from the orphanage and raised her with her own two children. Unfortunately, her husband did not want my mother in the home. He resented having another mouth to feed. He and his son constantly abused her verbally. The son harassed and physically abused her too.

My mother was a sickly child who suffered from malnutrition, rickets, Saint Vitus Dance, beriberi, rheumatic fever, and other diseases. She had so many ear infections that were ignored that she became hearing impaired. On one occasion while shaking uncontrollably, she bit off the end of her tongue. She only completed third grade and left school because of numerous health problems.

Her father took her back at the age of twelve because his new wife wanted help with the house and their combined children. She was very cruel to my mother. She fed her own children well and kept a padlock on the refrigerator so my mother could not get any food other than what she rationed out to her.

She was constantly verbally and emotionally abused in addition to the physical cruelties. On one occasion, her mother poured hot water on her head and then laughed at her.

At the age of fifteen, she met my father. She was starved for love. They were married after only two weeks. Both had violent fathers, and both were starved for the love of someone who would be nice to them. I think they were both too needy and had unrealistic expectations of one another. I doubt they had ever experienced love—other than what my father's mother showed him.

They married during the Depression and had four children in rapid succession. My father was mostly unemployed during those difficult days. I'm sure the stress level in our house was very high most of the time.

My mother aborted the fifth and sixth babies and had tried unsuccessfully to abort me. I was the last live birth they had. My mother told me that after having three children, my father told her that if she got pregnant again, he would leave her and the children. She became panicky because she had no work experience and had not even completed grade school. My father found a man in the city to come to our house and abort me. The man failed to kill me, and that created huge problems for my parents. My mother aborted the two babies after me. The abortions left her with a great deal of anger and guilt, and it followed her to her grave.

In 1944, my thirteen-year-old brother was diagnosed with terminal colon cancer. He died in 1947, just after his fifteenth birthday, and his death left an aftermath of grief and a path of destruction that has lasted more than sixty years. In other chapters, I will share how each member of the family suffered permanent damage by this grief.

My mother decided that my brother's death was her fault because it was God's punishment for "killing the babies." Her grief was inconsolable and resulted in forty years of severe depression and attempted suicides. She took that grief to the grave, believing she was responsible for his suffering and death. She hadn't had a great deal of joy in her life up to 1947, and from that day forward, she was more dead than alive. Alcohol and multiple drugs became a way of life. Mental illness became a safe haven away from reality.

As quite often happens when a child dies, my mother saw my dead brother as a saint. She could only remember what a good boy he was and constantly reminded the surviving siblings of what a perfect child he was. My mother built a shrine to her dead son in her heart and in her mind and worshipped there daily. Guilt, grief, and memories were all she had left.

In 1947, grief was thought to be a passing thing, and prolonged grief was not tolerated. Our friends and family certainly did not understand the depth of my mother's grief, and some were very critical. They believed she "should have been over that a long time ago." Some people avoided her because she was too depressing to be around, which alienated her even more and pulled her further inside herself.

My mother internalized her guilt and anger behind a very passive facade. This resulted in several physical ailments as well as a severe lifelong depression. She had never been allowed to show anger when she was growing up; anger was not tolerated, and girls were punished severely when they demonstrated anger. Ironically, they were punished for being angry by abusive, angry caregivers. It was okay for the males to be angry and show it physically, but girls were not permitted anger in any form. My mother learned to stuff her feelings at a very early age, and that continued throughout her life.

My mother had no self-esteem. She was condemned from birth to feel worthless. Her only role in life as far as she was concerned was being a burden. Throughout her childhood, she was an object of abuse. If something went wrong or the people around her were unhappy, it was her fault. She was never praised or appreciated.

The greatest joy she experienced in life was when she was pregnant or had a new baby. The only success she experienced in life was being a mother. Having babies or being pregnant made her feel worthwhile. Unfortunately, each new baby added stress to the family. When she started aborting the babies to save her marriage, she lost the feeling of success as a mother. When her son died of cancer and she took the blame, she turned against herself and brutally decided she was not even good at being a mother. She called herself a "murderer," and that label went with her to the grave. When people ask me when my mother died, I tell them she died in 1947, but wasn't buried until 1987.

I weep for my mother's life. She died at the age of seventy-five, and her life was filled with pain. She spent a great deal of time wishing she were dead. In later years, no matter how hard we tried to show her that we loved her, she did not believe it. She could not believe anyone could love her for herself. She was very difficult to be around in the last few years of her life. Some doctors said she was mentally ill. Perhaps she was, but is it any wonder? I'm not sure she was ever mentally well—from the day she was conceived.

Gloom in the Womb

Tiny Victims of Violence

What we believe about our self-worth and how we feel about life in general begins the moment we are conceived. For far too many children, that first impression is not only negative, but also very frightening. It can leave scars that last a lifetime. I am referring to unwanted children or those who survived an unsuccessful abortion. Their parents tried to kill them!

I am in favor of therapeutic abortions if performed for the right reasons. I am *not* in favor of abortions to end a pregnancy because the parents did not want a child of that sex. I am opposed to abortion as a method of birth control. That is ignorance at its highest point. I am violently opposed to unsafe abortions attempted by women who find themselves in a difficult situation because of an unwanted pregnancy. They run the risk of serious infection or death.

My main reason for opposing self-performed abortions and those done by untrained health professionals is because of the damage done to the unborn child's psyche. From the moment of conception, he or she was unwanted. Then her mother, or someone else just as unqualified, tries to kill him or her in the womb. The child eludes the hunter out to kill him or her and survives the abortion only to be born unwanted and unloved. From the moment of conception, the life script for that child says, "Don't live!" or "You are an unwanted burden!" It is difficult to have any sense of self-worth unless that message can somehow be reversed.

Perhaps L. Ron Hubbard wrote the strongest indictment I have heard against attempted abortions in *Dianetics*. He states, "Once a child is conceived, no matter how 'shameful' the circumstances, no matter the mores, no matter the income, that man or woman who would attempt an abortion on an unborn child is attempting a murder which will seldom succeed and is laying the foundation of a childhood of illness and heartache."

He adds, "If a person knows he has committed this crime against a child who has been born, he should do all possible to have that child 'cleared' as soon as possible after the age of eight and in the meantime should treat that child with all the decency and courtesy possible in order to keep the engram out of restimulation. Otherwise he may send that child to an institution for the insane."

His strongest statement follows: "A proportion of allegedly feebleminded children are actually attempted abortion cases whose engrams place them in fear paralysis or regressive palsy and which command them not to grow but to be where they are forever."

That is pretty strong and very frightening. We must love our children from the moment of conception (not birth) if we want them to be healthy physically, emotionally, and spiritually. If we attempt to kill our children in the womb and they survive, they will be born with damaged spirits and no self-worth. They will have huge holes in their souls! They could spend their lives in pain and drift from one form of illness to another. Unless there is an opportunity for healing, they will spend their lives apologizing for being alive and trying to prove that it is okay that they survived their mothers' attempts to kill them.

My strongest reason for opposing crudely performed abortions that fail to kill the child is based upon my own personal experience and that of my mother. I am a failed abortion, and this has had a significant impact on every day of my life. The knowledge that my parents attempted to have me aborted might not have been so traumatic if I had only heard it once or twice. I heard it constantly from the time I was a small child. I still hear it today—fifty-five years later. They would say, "We tried to kill her, but she didn't have the courtesy to die!" I was told I should not have been born and that I was one too many in an already overburdened family during the Depression.

My father had a standing joke that he used when he introduced me to friends and neighbors. "She was my last mistake. I told her mother we should shoot her and save the milk and raise hogs on the money we'd save. At least we could shoot the hogs, and we'd have something to eat." It was always a great joke to him, and he did not realize the impact it had on me.

Not everyone he told that joke to appreciated it as a joke, however. To those who never had any children or lost their children prematurely, it was an appalling statement. One couple said, "We would give anything in this world to have a daughter like her to love and love us in return. You are a very lucky man!"

And, of course, what added to the hurt of a serious attempt to get rid of me was the knowledge that my mother sold her breast milk when I was born to a local hospital. She said, "It paid good money, and we really needed the money." She would pump out her breasts during the day, put it in containers, and take it to the hospital for money. I'm not sure what I was given in exchange for her milk, but several doctors have told me that my numerous bone and joint problems are attributed to inadequate diet in the womb and throughout early childhood.

I got really angry with her a couple of months before she died, and exploded with the statement, "I can understand why you didn't want another child, and I can even understand why you felt you needed to get rid of me, but I don't understand why you couldn't just make the best of it. Even more important, why couldn't you have loved and accepted me and let me know that it was okay that I was alive? And why did you have to tell me over and over again that you tried to get rid of me?" I hurt her very deeply, and of course, she never had an answer, but I had to ask the question.

Scientific researchers are learning more and more each day about the experiences of the baby in the womb. Whatever affects the mother physically, emotionally, and spiritually affects the baby and leaves a memory of joy or sorrow. If they live in a peaceful, loving, safe environment, they interpret their world that way. If they are wanted and valued by their parents, they will have positive, healthy self-esteem when they are born.

Unfortunately, not all babies live in the womb in peace and love. Some are conceived in what is already a war zone in a dysfunctional family. These tiny people become victims of violence even before they are born and will probably continue to be victims of violence after they are born. Even when others are not abusing them, they may be abusing themselves because they believe they should not be alive.

If the fetus is as alert and sensitive as scientists say, then they experience a wide range of violence. Some pregnant women's mates punch them. Some women try to hurt themselves in an attempt to end the pregnancy. Some couples fight and argue loudly while the mother is pregnant. Some mothers abuse alcohol and drugs while pregnant, while others have such poor nutrition that it is insufficient to feed himself or herself or the baby.

Then there is the whole range of unwanted babies. There are those who never wanted a baby at all. There are those who consider a baby to be too great a financial burden. There are those who fantasized that a baby would mend their deteriorating relationship, but it had the opposite effect. Some parents wanted a boy or a girl and learned early in the pregnancy that the mother was pregnant with a child of the unwanted sex (boys are usually preferred). There are those who have all the children they want and do not want another child. Some babies are the result of unprotected sex or a night of drunken entertainment. They were never planned, they were not wanted, and if they survive, they will probably be unwanted and unloved. And like so many of us, they will start life with the life script of "Don't Live!"

There have been studies about depressed mothers and the effect on the fetus. The chemical makeup of the mother changes for better or worse as her mood changes. Those chemical changes affect her unborn child. The baby can become depressed and develop a depressed personality. Depending on the mother's state of mind when the child is born, she may interact with the baby in a depressed manner.

The baby will pick up on cues from the mother and may be more difficult to soothe. The mother may be depressed and interact negatively with her baby. Normal bonding will not take place. The mother and child never get close, and instead only irritate and depress each other. Depressed babies may become depressed toddlers. A troubled child who was traumatized in the womb can be incapable of intimacy or joy. Professional help will be needed to help the child move away from depression and develop self-worth.

My mother was not only an unwanted child, but she was also born to a severely depressed mother. My mother was a failed abortion. Her mother had lost four children in one week to diphtheria and had never grieved those losses. She became pregnant with my mother while still grieving. She had a miscarriage the year after my mother was born and died from a botched abortion two years after that.

At the age of two, my mother was considered so useless and unwanted that her father gave her to a Catholic orphanage. She was depressed all of her life and thus felt unloved and unwanted. That was her inheritance from her mother and that was the inheritance she passed down to me when I was born. I have struggled fifty years to achieve something that would overshadow the mistake of my birth. I have apologized the majority of my life for "not having the courtesy to die" when my parents tried to abort me. I became a people-pleaser, a caretaker, and an overachiever in an attempt to gain permission to be alive. I have spent most of my life depressed and have been suicidal. I have given and given to everyone who would take from me, and I have expected nothing in return. That only left me feeling angry and empty. What a terrible waste of a decent human being!

The things we do to our children in the womb and in childhood are frightening. If we continue to abuse and neglect them, we destroy any chance of a normal, healthy adult life. They are born to grieve just as we were born to grieve and just as our grandchildren will be born to grieve. Happiness and serenity will elude us if we are unable or unwilling to heal the wounds of the past.

Unwanted children also present a frightening picture for the future of our world. We hear about mass murderers or serial killers who were severely abused as children. They grow up as angry, self-destructive people who take their revenge out on innocent victims. They are violent, hurtful people who probably never experienced the feeling of being loved or wanted.

Our nation will have to face some serious problems in the coming years. There are those who were damaged by being unwanted at birth. There are those babies who were born addicted to cocaine and needing special care. We do not know yet what the ramifications of that problem will be. There are increasing numbers of children who have been damaged by inadequate or abusive day-care providers. There are homeless children and children from broken homes. There is unemployment, poverty, and other social ills. Last, but not least, are all the children being born with AIDS and or are orphaned by this terrible disease.

We always seem to be one day late and many dollars short when it comes to caring for our children. Children are the most precious and priceless gift that America has, but our investment in them is often too little and too late. We need to rethink our priorities and realize that if we do not invest in our children, we will be spending it on more prisons and hospitals to house those damaged souls who have committed serious crimes. Perhaps we need to spend a little less on the military and a little more on the homes and streets of America.

An Assault for a Lifetime

Surviving Personal Violence

Words like mugging, in-home invasion, murder, rape, child abuse, battery, homelessness, hunger, cold, abandonment, disease, disability, terminally illness, destitution, and post-traumatic stress disorder sound short and simple. They are not pleasant words or happy words. To the average person, the words do not carry the terror that they do for the victim. The full impact of how a life is affected by crime is unappreciated and undervalued by much of society. It is even more gravely unappreciated and misunderstood by those in authority such as government officials, health care providers, clergy, employers, etc.

We turn on the news or pick up the newspaper and read articles about people being mugged in broad daylight. Perhaps we have a moment of sadness or say a little prayer for that victim, but we might not give the story any more thought.

In 1972, I learned that there is no such thing as a simple crime. I was mugged at my place of employment while I was managing a two hundred-unit high-rise for the elderly. The injury to my leg was simple, and I seemed to recover quickly, but five years later my leg became unstable and required surgery.

It was to be a simple surgery to reattach the knee joint. However, I picked up a hospital staph infection and grew many dangerous bacteria. The infection invaded the bone, which resulted in chronic osteomyelitis. That was the beginning of the end for my health, my marriage, my employment, my insurance coverage, my financial security, and so much more.

The leg remained open, draining, and infected for eight years. In an attempt to fix the problem, the doctors removed a cup of bone from my hip and grafted it into my leg. The graft did not take, and my hip remained open and infected for three years. The doctors put a graft from my good leg in the infected leg. The infection ate through the graft and left me with circulation problems in my "good" leg.

I had a total of thirteen surgical procedures from that mugging, but nothing worked. I had to fight with worker's comp to get my medical bills paid, and they quit paying for my very expensive antibiotics. They quit paying for my dressings, and I had to use sanitary napkins on my leg and hip. The antibiotics were in such high doses that I had frequent diarrhea and vomiting. My weight dropped as low as seventy-five pounds. I was too weak to do much of anything.

If I bought groceries, I could not pay all of my

utility bills. One car was repossessed. One car I bought for $250 had the engine drop out at a stop sign. I had many medical appointments. I was constantly bombarded by collection agencies. My medical specialist informed me I could not make an appointment unless I paid cash. I needed X-rays and other tests, but I had no money.

At one point, I ran a high fever for several days. They packed me in ice but could not find the right drug to slow the infection. I was told I was dying and that I should tell my children to prepare them.

For better or for worse, in sickness and in health, until death do us part. I had known my husband since I was ten years old, and we had been married for twenty-seven years. I learned that he could not stand diseased, disabled people with open wound. I spent many months in the hospital, and he could not bear to be around me. I knew I could not live with someone who could not touch me. My family disapproved of divorce even though we were not Catholic. I made the only decision that seemed to be left to me. On Easter in 1979, I decided to end my life, believing it would be better for everyone. I did not complete the act because my sixteen-year-old daughter would have found my body, and I could not leave her with that burden.

I went into counseling and finally reached the important decision that no man is worth it. For that matter, no person who brings only pain and suffering is worth it. However, if we have been raised in abusive, male-dominant families, we follow that belief system until we find help.

I filed for divorce and lost even more than I had lost up to that point. My soon-to-be ex canceled my health insurance and life insurance. I had to pay a penalty for life insurance and could not get health insurance for ten years because of my physical problems. The life insurance company told me that my chances of dying young were more probable than the average. We owned much property, and a judge gave my ex all of the property—and gave me the mortgage for one of the properties. On the day of the divorce, I did not even have a vehicle. I was on a home IV program. The judge gave the family van to my ex.

I could not get the help I needed. To appeal the divorce decision, I had to pay an attorney ten thousand dollars, and they felt I would lose anyway. I did not even have five hundred dollars. I begged my worker's comp agent to pay my bills to no avail. Was that justice?????? Absolutely not—but it was reality!

I am now a retired senior citizen, and many wonderful things have happened in my life. My body is still paying the price for that day in 1972, and I have disabilities I would not have had if that had not happened to me.

- I wrote a devotional that was published in 1986 in hardcover and in paperback in 1991. I was on a speaking tour for three years. I spent two years as an emergency chaplain at a local hospital.

- Prior to the mugging, I was a nighttime street counselor in a major city for six years.
- Professionally I was an alcohol/drug/grief counselor. I have learned much about grief over the years.

My life is rewarding and full. When I hear about crime victims, they are not simple, short-term stories. They can affect entire lifetimes and the lives of many others. Unfortunately, I have met many people who never really recovered from violence. They still carry the scars. No one was ever arrested or held responsible for the mugging.

Loss of a Baby

A Love Cut Short

The greatest personal loss is the loss of a child. It does not matter if we lose a child in infancy, childhood, or adulthood. It seems cruel and unnatural for children to precede us in death.

When we lose a parent, we lose part of our past, and much around us changes because of that loss. When we lose a child, we lose an important part of our future. Hopes and dreams are obliterated before our eyes, and we feel a profound sense of loss. We lose our sense of balance and look for someone to blame. Too often, we come full circle. The grief is so profound that many people go to their graves with it.

I lost my third child to miscarriage during the sixth month, and it started a self-destructive grief that lasted twenty-two years. I had two daughters less than three years of age, and I was too exhausted physically and emotionally for another pregnancy. Unfortunately, instead of receiving the support from my mother and other important family members, I was accused of getting rid of the baby. I believed that myself.

The day I went to the hospital, I was running a 105-degree temperature and was hemorrhaging. The baby survived for nine days. I was kept flat in a hospital bed and fed a light diet so that I would not have to sit up to go to the bathroom. Every day, they did a rabbit test to determine if the baby was still alive. Then they would come in and joyfully announce that the baby was well and all would be fine.

The second day of my hospitalization, my parents left the state for a vacation. I heard nothing from them until my fourth day in the hospital when I received a letter from my mother. I was shocked by the contents of her letter. She started out by saying that she hoped I had lost my poor, unwanted little gift because the worst thing that could happen to that baby would be for it to have me as a mother. She called me a murderer and told me that someday when I sat at the bedside of one of my children dying of cancer, I would know that God was punishing me for killing my baby. Then she disowned me.

At the time I received the letter, I did not know about my mother's abortions. That had been a well-kept secret when I was a child. I also was unaware that she blamed herself for my brother's death and believed that it was punishment for the abortions. I knew she had tried unsuccessfully to abort me, but I had been unaware of the other two.

I was deeply hurt by her letter. At that point, my

baby was still alive. I had done nothing to cause a miscarriage. Eventually, I accepted the name my mother had called me—*murderer*—and ended up with twenty-two years of unresolved grief.

On the ninth day, I sat up on a bedpan and the baby fell out. The doctor did a dilation and curettage procedure, and explained why I had lost the baby. I told him I did not want to know anything about it, not even the sex of the baby. When he discharged me the next day, he handed me an envelope and said, "Someday you may want to know about your baby. The details are in here." I went home with empty arms and began the long, destructive grief process.

My parents disowned me for murdering my baby. My husband was not in touch with his feelings or mine. I felt as if he was relieved because it would be one less expense. In the fifties, the impact of the loss of a child through a miscarriage was not understood. Friends gave me the usual advice: "You can have more children," "At least you have two other healthy children," "It is better off dead," and "God needed another little angel in heaven." With no one to turn to, I turned my grief inward and accepted the blame for the baby's death.

I was so hurt by my mother's letter. I vowed that no one would ever hurt me that much again. I put her letter and the envelope from my doctor in a dresser drawer. I read her letter every week for two years, and then once a month for many years. Each time I read it, I would become angry all over again. I would remind myself that people could never be trusted. I left the envelopes in my dresser for twenty-two years before the grief was resolved.

When a woman loses a baby through miscarriage or at birth, she can always find reasons to blame herself. Perhaps she did not take good enough care of herself. Maybe she did not want the baby badly enough. Was she being punished for something she had done wrong? From there, her thinking goes from guilt to fear. Will I ever get pregnant again? Will I ever carry a child to full term? Will I ever have a healthy baby, or will the next one die too?

Medical personnel and well-meaning friends gravely underestimate the impact of child loss, and how the child was a major part of the woman's physical, emotional, and spiritual life for however long she carried the child. Women do not recover from this loss as simply as having a tooth extracted. We cannot simply forget it and get on with life. The loss must be recognized with its full impact, and it must be fully grieved if we are to recover.

I want to share how the loss of my child was resolved after twenty-two years. I believe we have many opportunities to resolve the hurts and grief in our lives, but we choose not to deal with them unless we are forced by circumstances beyond our control. When we reach a point where we can no longer manipulate our way out of dealing with these issues, then perhaps we can start the healing process.

I was forced to deal with my loss in a significant and powerful way. I was apprehensive, but it became one of the best experiences in my life. I was a volunteer emergency chaplain at a hospital for three years. I was on call the hospital from eight o'clock P.M. until eight o'clock in the morning for any emergencies that required the services of a chaplain. We also went out with the police and fire departments for death notifications. Initially, the job as emergency chaplain was a requirement of training I was taking in clinical pastoral education (CPE). It was so rewarding that I stayed on long after the required six weeks.

One night while I was on duty, a six-week-old baby was brought into the hospital. She was a victim of sudden infant death syndrome (SIDS), although she had not yet been pronounced dead. The parents were led into the family room while the medical staff worked on the baby. I was called to be with the parents. The baby had not yet been baptized, so I baptized the baby and returned her to the family.

After a while, the medical staff came to advise the parents that their baby girl was dead. They wanted the opportunity to hold her before she was taken to the morgue. They brought her into the family room gave her to the parents. They took the baby with the morgue tag already attached to her toe and cradled her in their arms. They stroked her hair and body and spoke softly to her. It looked as natural as any parents with a living infant. The difference, of course, was that these parents were saying good-bye to their baby.

The mother turned to me and said, "Will you hold our baby for a few minutes?" I took the baby into my arms and felt very strange. It was as if I had been catapulted back in time—twenty-two years—to losing my own child. I felt as if I was embracing the baby I had lost but had never grieved. I could let the baby go. There was no longer a need to hold on. I knew it was okay to let go. I knew I was not responsible for the loss of my child.

The baby's mother thanked me for holding their baby and said to me softly, "I can tell two things about you: I can tell you are a mother yourself, and I can tell that you too have lost a baby. You held her so gently and so tenderly. Thank you."

I sat there with the parents holding their baby for two hours. At first, I thought it was strange, but as I watched the parents, I realized it was the healthiest way for them to deal with their loss. When their baby was born just six weeks earlier, they had greeted her and welcomed her into the world. Now, they were saying good-bye in the most loving way they could. They had begun the process of grieving in a healthy, supportive way.

Too often, when a child is lost in infancy, the body is whisked away quickly by the medical staff. Then, in many cases, the father, pastor, or well-meaning relative quickly has the child buried in order to "spare the mother." If she never has a chance to say good-bye, her grief can be prolonged indefinitely. Even when a baby has serious physical deformities, the mother needs to view her beloved child rather than try to imagine what the baby looked like. The mother will have the strength to deal with the baby's deformities much more readily than wondering about it. She also needs time to say good-bye.

My experience in that family room had a profound affect on my life from that point on. My unresolved grief after twenty-two years was resolved that evening as I shared the grief of those parents with their baby. When I got off duty, I went home and took both envelopes out of my dresser drawer. I tore up my mother's letter, and I finally opened the envelope from my doctor. I learned that the child I lost was my first son. I also learned that I had a severe virus that had caused the loss of my baby. If the baby had lived, he would have been profoundly retarded and probably institutionalized. I was finally able to stop blaming myself for that loss and to forgive my mother for the hurt she had caused me.

I needed to understand that my mother's attitude about the loss of a child had been seriously tainted by her own experiences and by the fact that she had voluntarily aborted two children. She had honestly believed that a healthy woman would never have lost a child in miscarriage unless she had done something to cause it. That had been reality for her, and she had transferred the burden of her reality to my loss.

Unfortunately, I had never opposed my mother during my entire lifetime. I had never seriously questioned whether she was right or wrong. It had not been difficult to convince me that I was a murderer since I had low self-worth from the day of my conception. I was, after all, alive only because my parents had failed in their attempt to have me aborted. I had been reminded of that all of my life—verbally and emotionally.

This is a good example of why we need to understand our own personal histories. If I had known the complications of my mother's life, I would have understood her violent reaction to my loss. It might not have become a personal burden. Perhaps my loss could have been grieved without the added burden of guilt and shame, and the label of "murderer."

There are many groups available for parents who lose children. There are special groups for parents of SIDS deaths, for parents of murdered children, for those whose children are killed by a drunk driver, and so on. Not all doctors or clergy members take the time to recommend these groups, and some people are just not aware such groups exist. It is important to find the kind of support that is special in each case. If the hospital staff does not suggest this option, we need to pursue it for ourselves. We need help to grieve our special losses.

As a final point of interest to this story, let me tell you about the doctor who insisted I take the envelope he provided for me the day I left the hospital. He had been in Auschwitz and had survived primarily because he played an instrument. He had been a part of the band that played music for the incoming prisoners before they were sent to the gas chamber.

Right after I lost my baby, he was going on a vacation to Poland to see his mother. They had not seen each other since World War II. He was truly excited about his visit. Tragically, the plane crashed before he got to see his mother. He was a wonderful, kind doctor with a sense for the good in others, even when they could not see it.

If he had not provided me with that envelope, it would have been difficult—if not impossible—to get the information that was so important for my healing. I am convinced that God takes care of us even when we do not recognize it. I believe that the doctor giving me the envelope, my saving it for so long, and that night in the emergency room were made possible by the love of God. I believe we have many opportunities to resolve our grief. If we do not, God backs us into a corner. I am most grateful for that gift of love.

The Wounded Child

The Child Who Never Grows Up

The wounded child within us can remain unhealed for many years, and possibly for a lifetime. Some bury the hurt very securely beneath a veil of traumatic amnesia because they are unable to deal with the pain. The reality of the hurt is so real and the betrayal of the one who hurt them is so terrible that they cannot deal with it at that point in their life.

Unfortunately, if the wounded child remains unhealed, it is impossible to be healthy emotionally, physically, and spiritually. We can manage to function on a daily basis and may not be aware that we are not well, and serenity will elude us because of the wounded child within us. Sometimes we bury the terrible secrets that are too scary for the conscious mind to deal with.

I read an article in the newspaper about a thirty-year-old woman whose childhood was triggered by a glimpse of her own daughter. The memory that was triggered was the molestation and murder of her eight-year-old friend twenty years earlier. Her own father had taken his daughter and her friend to run errands. On his way, he stopped along the roadside and raped her friend. The little friend got out of the van and crouched in terror. The father picked up a rock and bashed the girl's skull as his daughter watched in horror.

This memory was buried for twenty-one years. As a young child witnessing such a horrible act, she could not deal with it in her conscious mind. She deeply buried it to protect herself. Her own daughter bore a striking resemblance to her murdered friend, and as she watched her, the memory came flooding back. She also remembered repeated sexual abuse by her father. She reported the incident to authorities, and her father was convicted twenty-one years after the crime.

Perhaps we are fortunate that we suffer loss of memory from traumatic events. Sometimes we do not remember any part of a tragedy. At other times, we recall bits and pieces a little at a time. As long as the memories are buried deeply within our wounded child, we do not deal with them. They continue to affect our daily lives in a profound way, even though we are not aware of it. We never know when or how the memory of our wounded child will be triggered. It may be something very simple and seemingly unrelated, or it may be something similar that triggers our memory.

If we suppress our memories and continue to protect the suppression of those memories, a part of it may be triggered without us being consciously aware of what is happening. We may become physically ill or severely depressed but honestly believe nothing is bothering us. We may staunchly defend our wellness when questioned by doctors or friends. Although we are still protecting our wounded child by burying those memories at a subconscious level, we are paying the price with our bodies, minds, and spirits.

I recently experienced a flashback that I was totally unprepared to deal with. When I finally realized what was happening to me, I was amazed by the intensity of my feelings. It crippled me for more than a week. It even invaded my dreams.

The event that triggered my memory was a simple gift to my eighty-three-year-old father. He lived alone 1,700 miles from me and could still care for himself. He was forced to put his twelve-year-old dog to sleep because of illness, and was grieving the loss with great difficulty. He said he wanted another dog, and being a caretaker I found him one. I called him from the pet shop to make sure he really wanted another dog. When he said yes, I bought the dog and flew down to Arizona.

The dog was four months old and had been confined to a small cage for her entire life. She was accustomed to going potty on shredded newspaper. She was full of energy and in need of training. I explained that to my father several times.

I told him he would have to keep her in the fenced yard until she learned some simple commands. On the second day, he let the dog out in the front yard in the unfenced area. She took off to explore the area. When he finally caught her, he gave her a beating and swore at her over and over again. For several days after that, he kept saying "Goddamn stupid bitch—you'll either learn or I'll beat you to death." Each time he repeated it, I cringed and started feeling sick.

This went on for more than a week. Each time the dog committed a transgression, he became hostile and abusive, and I became very uneasy. I started waking up in the middle of the night in a cold sweat. I finally realized that I was experiencing a flashback to my own childhood. The words and actions my father was using on the dog were all too familiar. He had been the same when I was a child. I was so terrified of him that I would wet my pants just thinking about what he would do if I did something wrong. Then he would punish me for what I did wrong and for wetting my pants.

Each time he started yelling at the dog or hit her, I became that small, terrified child. I felt so helpless and frightened. As a child, that fear had completely immobilized me. I had to remind myself that I was no longer that helpless, frightened child whose life seemed to be in peril. I realized I was feeling as small and helpless as that little puppy in the presence of a much greater force. I decided there was no way I could go home and leave that defenseless puppy behind.

Fortunately, my father decided he did not want the dog. I took over the care of the dog for the remaining two weeks until I could take her home with me. She had already become so frightened of my father that she would not go up to him when he tried to be nice to her. He opened the door one day to let her in the house, but she would not come in until I stood between him and the door. In a short time, she had learned to crouch in fear and shame. It was pitiful to see.

I was amazed by how intensely the incident affected me. I did not stop having the nightmares until I decided to take the dog home with me. Once I took over the care of the dog and kept her in my room at night, the fear stopped. It took a lot more time to recover from the memory of that frightened, helpless child. It was strange to feel so incapacitated after so many years. Once I knew the dog was safe, I felt safe again.

Even though I am an independent adult with grown children of my own, I still pussyfoot around my father to avoid provoking his wrath. Although I confront him a great deal more than anyone else, I still put up with more than I should. Since he can be very volatile, I choose my words carefully when I criticize him. He is still the controlling parent, and I am still the frightened child who obeys out of fear rather than respect.

The wounded child buried deeply inside my second brother stayed there for thirty-six years. He finally killed himself because he could no longer bear the pain of everyday living. He never received sufficient help to understand his wounded child. The death of our older brother seriously damaged him. From that day on, his life was totally dysfunctional. Alcohol, drugs, mental illness, prison, and numerous suicide attempts became a way of life until he successfully ended his life on the anniversary of my other brother's death. The unhealed, wounded child caused his death.

The wounded child in my mother took a terrible toll on her life, and all the lives she touched. Since she was unwanted at conception and was considered a burden after birth, the wounded child grew larger with all the negative imprinting from the moment of birth until her death. It was like a cancer that causes terrible, excruciating pain, but there is no cure for it. She lived most of her tragic life before the world realized how much damage had been done. She inherited the grief from her own mother who had lost four children prior to her own birth. She gradually escaped into mental illness after my brother did. When she died, she felt as unloved as she must have felt the day she was born.

The wounded child never leaves us. It affects us every day in profound ways unless we are willing to work aggressively to heal it. To heal the wounded child, we have to understand him or her first. Opening the floodgates can cause a great deal of pain. We must want wholeness more than anything else. We must be willing to go through the pain of discovery and the joy of recovery. There will be times when we feel so torn apart by our memories that it hardly seems worth it. To survive the discovery process, we will need good counselors and supportive friends. It will not be easy, but it will be worthwhile. Whether you are eighteen or eighty, it is worth the time and the effort. Serenity is waiting at the end of the long, dark tunnel of discovery.

The wounded child manages to survive in adulthood one day at a time by clinging to the hope that someday he or she will be worthy in the eyes of the parents. If the child has never allowed himself to become a separate person, he or she will continue to be the parent's child. Repressed memories of put-downs are a ticking time bomb. The child never feels good and never changes his or her lifestyle. Some of these children spend their entire lifetimes waiting to hear their parents' words of love, acceptance, or approval. When the parent dies, these children feel angry and cheated. Or some, like my brother, will give up waiting for acceptance and get lost in the confusion of mental illness or suicide. It is a tragic ending to a lifetime of suffering and waiting.

I spent my first fifty years of my life doing things that I thought would make me worthy in the eyes of my parents. I was alive only because I was a failed abortion. I wanted to convince my mother that it was okay that she had been unsuccessful in her attempt to get rid of me. I felt it would have been better for me, and everyone else, if I had never been born or had died as an infant. Since that did not happen, I tried to prove to my parents that my life was worth the space it took up on this earth.

I was the only child to graduate from high

school and go on to college. I completed many special programs and became a certified chemical dependency counselor. I became a licensed multiple-housing manager with a specialty in the elderly field. I was given the humanitarian award for citizen of the year in my city. I was involved in a children's rights legislative committee. I became a nighttime street crisis counselor and served as an emergency chaplain for two years.

My first book was published in 1986, and I wrote a book of poems, thinking my mother would like them. I was constantly striving to achieve the one great accomplishment that would earn me some sense of worth in my mother's eyes. I was a full-fledged caretaker and people pleaser and had been since my brother died in 1947. As the family rescuer, I would paint myself bright red like an ambulance and go out at any time of day or night for family emergencies. There were a lot of emergencies involving my mother, my brother, and his family.

I tried to achieve the "right to life" I had been denied since conception. My mother could not see beyond her own grief and low self-worth. Sometimes she was critical of me because she said I was trying to "be better than anyone else in the family." I actually considered that a valid criticism and believed that once again I had failed to prove what a nice, intelligent person I was. Whenever she criticized my achievements, I crouched a little lower and felt more ashamed. She found one poem in my book with a minor reference to my childhood, and she did not like it, which negated the entire book.

It was unrealistic to have such high expectations for someone who had no self-worth. She could not give me what she did not have, but I desperately needed to feel that it was all right that I had survived. I kept trying, and it took fifty years to recover.

I realize now that I do not need permission from anyone for the right to live and breathe and be happy. The fact that I was born will always be my birthright. I need to accept, love, and appreciate myself because no one else can give that to me unless I first have it for myself. Unfortunately, that is a difficult place to reach unless the wounded child has had time to heal. It is amazing that a parental injunction "DIE! We don't want anymore children" became a lifelong message. When my parents said, "You do not deserve to live because you are an unwanted burden," it became deeply ingrained in my psyche.

We need to work aggressively to deal with our wounded child much earlier in our lives so we do not spend half of a century waiting for permission to live abundantly. We need to do this so that no life is lived as tragically as my brother who committed suicide after thirty-six years of unresolved grief.

Hidden Grief

The Silent Killer

Each of us grieves differently. Sometimes we do not allow ourselves to show our grief, and sometimes others prohibit us from expressing our grief. One thing is for certain: a loss not grieved does not simply go away. We can continue to bury it deeper until it is buried in our subconscious mind, but it does not go away. It is like a battery-operated radio that has been uncared for. The batteries are locked in that radio for so long that they begin to leak acid. The acid slowly eats away at the radio from the inside. Eventually there will be so much damage that the radio will be useless.

When we bury our grief, we are much like that radio. The wounds remain unhealed and slowly secrete acid that eats away at us from the inside. It makes even larger holes in our souls. We may not recognize that anything is wrong, but serenity will continue to elude us. We never feel really good, but we might not feel badly enough to do anything about it.

When I was a nighttime crisis counselor, I received a call from a woman who was concerned about her nineteen-year-old niece. She believed she was suicidal and recently became anorexic. Her niece had been failing for nearly a year, and the aunt was afraid she would kill herself.

I asked if the girl had had any significant losses in her life. The aunt said, "Well, yes, but that was when she was twelve! That was seven years ago."

I asked the aunt to tell me about the loss.

When the girl was twelve, she was responsible for her nine-year-old brother. He asked if he could play with the neighbor. She agreed and let him go next door. The neighbor was showing her brother his father's gun when it accidentally discharged and killed her brother. They were the only children in the family.

When I told the aunt that I suspected that the unresolved grief from her brother's death was killing the girl, the aunt said, "That can't be! She was just fine after his death. She was happy and healthy, and she got straight A's. She was just the sweetest, most trouble-free teenager anyone could ask for. She came through that whole situation great!"

I probed a little further and asked about the parent's reaction to the boy's death. She explained how awful it was because he was their only son. Her niece felt responsible at the time. It took the parents a long time to get over it.

I told her that her niece probably had not gotten over it yet.

She was sure that could not be the problem "after all these years."

When I told her that my brother had killed himself thirty-six years after the death of his sibling, and on the anniversary date of his death, she finally believed me. I urged her to get counseling for her niece as quickly as possible to explore the unresolved grief.

I also counseled an eighty-five-year-old woman who had carried her grief for more than forty years. She had been angry with her husband for forty years, and he had been dead for thirty years. They could not have children of their own, but had taken in a newborn baby girl through foster care. They had her for three years and were attempting to adopt her. At that time, if you took a child in as a foster child, you were not allowed to adopt him or her. Both parents had grown to love this child as their own. The father worshipped the little girl. He would take her for a walk each day all dressed up with her hair in ribbons to show her off. She was his pride and joy.

The social worker took the child away and placed her with another couple. The husband went into a profound state of grief over the loss of Missy. The wife felt her husband should have been able to do something to stop the county from taking the child away. The couple's communication deteriorated. In her grief, she blamed him, and never forgave him for the loss of that little girl.

She wanted to adopt another child, but he refused. He destroyed all the pictures of Missy and all of her personal items. It was as if she had never existed. He would not allow anyone to talk about her or mention her name. She had hidden one little picture for all those years. She asked me to come to her room in the nursing home, and she showed me the picture. It took a long time to dig out the carefully hidden picture. She cried as if the injury to her soul had just happened, but it had been forty years.

The husband died much younger than he probably would have if he hadn't carried such a burden. The wife became paralyzed shortly after the loss of the little girl. She had so many health problems that she needed constant care. I believe that both of them lost the will to live when they lost their child. Instead of comforting each other, they turned inward. They started dying one day at a time. I imagine she carried her grief to the grave. When I talked with her that night, her grief was all she had left. She wasn't willing to let go of it.

Children have an even more difficult time resolving their grief. This happens for several reasons. First, children quite often feel somehow responsible when a loved one dies. They might think it happened because they were bad. They might have had bad thoughts or wishes about the person. Children think they have power over life and death and feel responsible, and quite often do not have the opportunities to express grief. Adults make the mistake of believing children are too young to be affected by the loss, and do not pay much attention to their need to be involved in the grief process.

If the parents are in such a state of grief, the children feel they have to "be strong" and "be good" so they do not cause their parents any more pain. The family may have already been so torn apart by the loss that the child stuffs the pain away and tries to keep up a happy appearance for the family. The parents assume this means that the child was not affected that much by the loss. Although this may surprise them, the parents are grateful to have one less "problem" to deal with. The child's grief gets put on hold, and although it is hidden from view, it can be devastating.

In the case of the girl whose brother was shot and killed, I'm sure many things were going on simultaneously that prevented her from resolving her grief. Although her parents did not mean to wound her even more than she was, they might have said, "Why did you let your brother go over there? You were supposed to take care of your brother, and now he is dead!"

The parents placed even more guilt on the child. She had to deal with the emotional impact of her parents losing their only son. Her parents' lives may have been so fractured that the girl felt she had to be almost perfect to prevent any more pain in their lives. That was a terrible burden at a time when she was hurting so much herself, and the pain within her must have been almost unbearable. I'm surprised she lasted seven years before falling apart.

When my brother died of cancer, I took the responsibility for his death, and for my family's pain.

He had been sick for so long, and my parents had been away from home so much to be with him. I just wished he would hurry up and die; when he died, I blamed myself. I thought my parents would be all right once he died, but our family situation became even worse. Part of my grief was masked by traumatic amnesia, but their grief went to their graves with them.

In my second brother's case, no one understood why he got into so much trouble. He was so self-destructive that his life was always in crisis. He suffered terribly during those thirty-six years that you could almost feel the pain vibrating off his body and spirit. It became exhausting to spend much time with him because he was saturated with depression and grief. Although it was a relief when he died, it was also a terrible loss. We had spent so much of our lives together. It was such a waste of a beautiful, creative human whose spirit was too crushed to survive.

If the pain my mother carried all of her life on the inside had been audible on the outside, the noise would have been deafening. It was painful to spend time with her because her spirit was so shattered. I always left her feeling physically, emotionally, and spiritually exhausted. I felt so sad and helpless in her presence. Her hidden grief killed her years before she was buried.

Traumatic Amnesia

When Circuits Overload

The definitions of traumatic amnesia range from very simple to very complex. For me, it has been simple to explain and difficult to recover from. My personal interpretation of traumatic amnesia is this: when the trauma in my life becomes too intense for me to cope with, my circuits overload and I lose my memory. This has happened to me more than once, and it has had a significant impact on my life. One occurrence was when I was eleven, and the other was when I was forty-two. I never recovered from the episode that occurred as a child. I still have no memory of the time preceding that traumatic amnesia.

I was eleven when my brother died of cancer. Our farm was far from hospital, and I was too young to visit him. I had not seen him for several months when his body was brought home to our little town for burial.

At the funeral, we had an open casket before and after the funeral service. At the end of the service, my mother took my hand and pulled me up to the casket. She told me to touch my brother's hand and "say good-bye to Buddy." As I touched his cold, bony hand, a shock went through my body. My mind went blank, and I was in a trance.

I did not believe it was really my brother. Buddy only weighed fifty pounds, his eyes were sunken, and his hair had turned snow white. I thought someone was pulling a terrible prank on my parents. I thought they had sent home someone else's body and that my brother was still alive somewhere.

During the year that my brother had been away from home, my parents were gone a majority of that time in order to be with him. My sixteen-year-old sister and my twelve-year-old brother took care of me. They did not always treat me kindly. They used to lock me in the dirt cellar underneath the kitchen floor. It was completely dark and cold and damp. There were no windows and no lights, and it had many creepy, crawly creatures.

As the months went by, my family became more and more difficult to relate to. The pressure of a dying child and the mounting medical bills took a toll on everyone. At first, I believed my brother would get well and come home. I thought my mother would come home to take care of me. As time passed, I began to doubt that he would ever come home.

I was frustrated by my sibling's caretaking, and I started wishing he would die soon so my parents could come back home. When he died, I thought it was because I had wished it. I sincerely believed that I had caused his death. As I watched my family deteriorate following his death, I felt responsible for all their pain.

From the moment I touched my dead brother's hand in the coffin, all memories of him left my mind. Sixty-four years after that day, I still have no memory of him. I have seen many pictures of him, and we played together with our sibling, but I cannot recall a single thing about him or even that he existed prior to that day. I have been told he was very kind to me and protective of me when we were growing up.

The only memory I have of this person who was my brother and playmate for ten years is that coffin scene and those white, stiff, cold, bony fingers. I have been unable to free any other memory of him since that day. It is like he never existed in my lifetime, but I know he did because his death obliterated my family. I have never recovered from traumatic amnesia, and perhaps I never will. I'm not even sure it would benefit me to remember something I have kept buried for so long.

My life was never the same after his death, and I often felt like a stranger in my own home. It was like everyone else was on the inside of the house, and all the doors and windows were locked. I was always looking in through a large picture window. I could see them and hear them, but they could not see me or hear me no matter how loudly I cried out. As I looked in, I could not understand why they did not notice I was missing. This scene or dream first appeared just a few months after my brother's funeral and before my twelfth birthday. Before my brother's death, I do not think I was really on the inside of that family, but after his death, I always felt locked out.

My first experience of traumatic amnesia did not upset me because I did not really understand what had happened for several years. My second experience was very frightening and could have had serious consequences. I completely pulled away from people and abandoned the support system that I needed.

The second episode happened three weeks after my forty-one-year-old sister-in-law killed herself. I had been visiting her that evening, and she was taking a lot of drugs and mixing them with alcohol. She had been to a new doctor the day before, and he had given her thirty amphetamines without knowing her physical or emotional background. She kept taking drugs to feel good and reach that high. I warned her several times that she was in danger of a fatal overdose. She just looked at me and said, "Vetsch, I don't really care! My family is all goofed up, and I'm tired of all the pain. I would just as soon be dead."

She was very depressed that night. My brother had been out of prison only a short time, her son had just gone back to prison, and she was concerned about what she considered some unhealthy choices her three daughters were making. My brother and sister-in-law were raising their two-year-old grandson because of difficulties their youngest daughter was having. It was July 2nd, and my sister-in-law had not been invited to her family's annual reunion because of my brother's problems and unpredictable behavior. That hurt her a great deal.

They had company that night, and everyone in the house, except the two-year-old and I, was stoned beyond reason. I was scheduled to enter the hospital the next day for a series of surgeries to correct the injuries from the mugging. I was in a great deal of physical pain and seemed to be accomplishing nothing in that house.

I begged my sister-in-law to stop risking her life, and then I went home since I could do no good there. I lived only a short distance from my brother's house, and when I got home, the telephone was ringing.

My brother said, "Vetsch, I know Jeanette is dead. They took her to the hospital, but I do not have a way to get there. I can't leave the baby alone."

I assured him I would be right over. I took one of my daughters along to stay with their grandson.

When we arrived at the hospital, we were ushered into a family room. Before long, a nurse, chaplain, doctor, and police officer came into the room. They told us she was dead. She had died of coronary and respiratory arrest.

I took my brother home and learned what had happened after I left. My sister-in-law was still trying to kill her emotional pain. Right after I left, she begged my brother to give her two hits of speed intramuscularly. He said he could not bear it when she cried, and he injected the speed. She felt sick and went over to the kitchen sink to throw up. Their water was set above the safety standard. The faucet came up over the sink and curved at the end. She got her head caught in the sink, and the scalding water burned the skin off one side of her face. My brother and his friends were too stoned to figure out how to get her head out from under the faucet. They dropped the phone and broke it while trying to call for help. They had to go to a neighbor's house. Their rescue attempts were a disaster.

I immediately accepted responsibility for the death of my sister-in-law. After all, if I had not left her that night, she would not have died. At the very least, there would have been a sober, responsible person in the house to provide emergency services. I carried guilt for her death for more than a year.

As I was talking to my brother that night, I started to cry. After all, she had been my best friend as well as my sister-in-law. We had dated together and had gone through a great deal together. My brother said very harshly, "Vetsch, don't you cry! I can take it if anyone but you cries. Someone has to be strong." I had become the caretaker in my family at a very young age and that role was expected of me.

So once again I stuffed my pain, notified his children of their mother's death, arranged her funeral, arranged with the governor's office for my nephew to be escorted from prison to her funeral, put my brother in the hospital for severe depression, and took care of their two-year-old grandson for a while. I canceled my surgery, postponed my own grief, and took care of everyone else. That is what is expected of family caretakers who practice the "be strong" rule of conduct.

A month after her death, I was physically and emotionally exhausted. I decided to take some time for myself and went to our cabin two hundred miles away. I told my husband and children I wanted to be left completely alone and warned that if anyone came to check on me or bothered me, I would take off in my car and just keep driving.

My leg had been open to the bone, draining, and infected for some time. I ran a fever regularly and took potent antibiotics to try to control the infection until I could reschedule surgery. I was physically, emotionally, and spiritually more exhausted than I can ever remember.

The cabin was twenty-five miles from a town and about four miles from the nearest telephone. There was no running water and no electricity. When I arrived, I somehow lost my purse and car keys. I was too exhausted to notice. I was so distraught that I slept most of the time.

When I was awake, I felt guilty for having left her. I was terribly angry with God for letting her die. I was eating poorly, and the potent antibiotics were making me more nauseated and giving me frequent diarrhea. My leg was a mess, and my fever was getting uncontrollable. I was getting even sicker than I was at home.

On the second day, I completely lost my memory. I tried to do some journaling every evening, but my world was like a huge void. I was so numb that when I walked to the outhouse, it was like walking through a dark, narrow tunnel. I could not remember my children's names or telephone numbers. I had put all of my medications into one convenient carrier, so there was no doctor's name or telephone number. I could not ignore the pain in my leg, but I could not have cared less about dressings and sterilization. I just didn't care.

I crossed off the first day on the calendar when I arrived because it is easy to lose track without a radio or television. I continued to cross the days off on the calendar. When it became too dark to see in the cabin, I would put another X on the calendar. I was sleeping most of the time, and the sludge of severe depression covered like a massive mudslide.

I struggled to remember who I was and what I was doing there. The more I struggled, the more confused I became. I could not have walked out for help because I would not have known where to go for help and because my leg was too badly infected to walk much farther than the outhouse. I had a car, but no keys.

I stayed in a state of numbness for six days and nights. Every time I woke up, I wanted to go back to sleep. I had gone to the cabin wishing I could just be dead like my sister-in-law, and perhaps I was hoping that would happen. Death seemed like the only way to end the physical, emotional, and spiritual pain.

I knew I was running out of pills. Something deep inside me finally started to get concerned about my welfare. I must have been getting concerned at an intellectual level because I certainly did not feel much of anything. I did not care about anything other than sleeping. I thought, *If only I could sleep forever and never wake up.* Every time I woke up, I was angry. It was as if waking up had disturbed the only peace I had ever known.

On the sixth day, I went for a short walk. I walked and tried to activate my memory. *There has got to be something in there to remember.* Then almost halfheartedly I said, "God wouldn't leave me in a mess like this." Suddenly, just having said the word, "God" I felt less alone and trapped. I had not given God a thought for six days because I had decided He either did not exist or had abandoned me when I needed Him most. I was so angry with my sister-in-law and myself that it was easier to blame God. After all, my sister-in-law was depressed. I stupidly left her that night, but where was God? Wasn't He supposed to be the guardian of fools? Wasn't He in charge of life and death? If anyone could have saved her, it should have been God.

When I recognized a power greater than myself, my mind started to clear. I went back to the cabin and started to write whatever came to my mind. A great deal of my anger, guilt, and grief started to pour out on the pages. I wrote for a while and searched for my keys. I left for home immediately because I realized I had been in a potentially serious situation back in the woods with no one to come to my aid.

When we suffer traumatic amnesia, we are often unaware of what is happening to us. We may need help and not realize it. It is important to reach out to others who can help us deal with our losses.

Thirty-Six Years of Grief

Resolved by Suicide

I want to share my second brother's reaction to our brother's death. His grief was so profound that he killed himself on the anniversary date of his death thirty-six years later.

When my older brother died, my other brother was thirteen. With less than two years between the boys, they were inseparable. I was too young to visit my brother in the hospital, but my brother and sister watched him suffer and deteriorate for a year. It was very difficult for them.

There was very little understood about the impact of a child's death to a family in 1947, and even less was known about the impact on the surviving siblings. In less than six months, my surviving brother was involved in juvenile delinquency. He began drinking, staying out all night, and generally getting into trouble with the law. He was out of control at a time when my parents were having great difficulties coping.

My mother was still suffering from profound grief

and considered her dead son a saint. Each time my surviving brother got into trouble, my mother would say, "It's too bad you didn't die instead of Buddy. He was a good boy and would have made us proud. You cause us nothing but trouble and shame." My brother heard that often enough that he believed it and adopted it as his life script. When he got stoned (which was often) or attempted suicide, he would always say, "I should have died instead of Buddy, and then the folks would be happy." As hard as I tried to convince him that it was not true, he believed it with every fiber of his being.

The first twelve years of his life, my brother had been my parent's favorite. When tragedy took the older son and the remaining son got into trouble, he lost that spotlight and plummeted to the bottom of the heap. In a way, he also lost his parents as well, and this was especially true with my mother because she felt she should have been kinder and more loving with the son who died. She felt that her older son had been punished many times for his younger brother's deeds. That was all a part of sainthood to idealize the dead child and find fault with the living.

She was in so much pain that she did not realize how deeply her distraught words would wound her remaining son. If she had known better, she would have done better. She was a very kind person who wanted nothing more than to be a good mother. She was already living with so much pain that I do not know where she would have put any more.

My brother's life was filled with pain, and he medicated his pain with alcohol and drugs. In the last year of his life, he was given ninety shock treatments and spent much of his time in the hospital. He died in November. Two weeks before his death, he said, "I can't make it until Christmas. I can't stay around any longer. I should have died instead of Buddy. When I'm dead, the folks can finally be happy. I owe them that." He was buried the day after Thanksgiving. He overdosed on the thirty-sixth anniversary of his brother's death.

Dying on the same date as my other brother was very important to him. He was paying a tribute to my parents because he felt like he should have died in his place. He became a victim of his own sibling grief and my mother's profound grief. He also became a victim of a society that did not understand or appreciate the high price we were all paying for unresolved grief.

We were all experiencing grief in different ways—and separate from one another. Aside from my dead brother's sainthood, we never discussed the tragedy of his death. We certainly never talked about feelings. We kept them inside.

I was twenty-two years old before I learned about my mother's abortions and the guilt she carried for my brother's death. We were an emotionally constipated family. My parents always said, "Don't cry! Be strong!" We were all crying on the inside and practicing the "Be strong!" lifestyle at the cost of our physical, emotional, and spiritual health.

Children get attention for being very good, very bad, or being sick. My brother could never have been good enough to compete with the sainthood of our dead brother, and he took the other path. His criminal activities increased. He spent time in prison, and he became a violent, frightening person. The more he got into trouble, the more criticism he drew from the family. He was disowned more than once which only added to his self-hatred.

His self-destructive lifestyle resulted in several suicide attempts. A year before he successfully killed himself, he shot himself in the head and wrist and slashed his wrists. I arrived in time to rescue him, but he truly wanted to die. He resented my rescue attempt. His wife had killed herself five years before, and he really wanted to die to get away from all the pain.

Grieving children often take responsibility for the death of a family member. My brother had the added burden of being told he should have died instead. In a short amount of time, that became a self-fulfilling prophecy for him. He spent his life dying a little more each day until his final death at the age of forty-nine.

Each child reacts differently to a death in a family. Some children seem to have almost no reaction, and people assume they are handling the situation well. They might be falling apart on the inside without ever showing it on the outside. Good communication is more important in a family after a loss than at any other time. Each family member must be allowed to show feelings and express them freely. If this is not possible before a loss, it will be especially difficult after a loss. Families need to grieve together as a unit rather than apart as my family did. Sorrow shared is sorrow diminished. Sorrow that is not expressed and shared festers and continues to cause pain. It can infect a person's entire life.

The greatest tragedy of my brother's life and death is that he was a truly gifted, intelligent person who had much to offer this world. He had a broad range of skills and a wonderful, humorous personality when it was not clouded by alcohol or drugs. Whatever he tried to do vocationally, he succeeded at for a short while. Then the "failure syndrome" crept back into his psyche. He would feel compelled to fit into the old mold of shame. The self-fulfilling prophecy always took over when it appeared that he might become successful at work or in a relationship. He was programmed for failure when his brother died, and he was never able to recover. He was always reminded that he should have died, which destroyed his belief that he had the right to live or be happy.

His few glimpses of happiness and success were always overshadowed by the guilt of being alive. He would go out and do something that was so repulsive that he would be disowned again, reinforcing his belief that he was no good, that he caused our mother only shame and that indeed he should have died instead of Buddy.

Although my brother could never allow himself to accept that he was a worthy person, he somehow saw so much potential in my life and was constantly bragging about me. He would embarrass me when he was talking to others in my presence about how smart I was. He would say, "This is my kid sister" and then go on and on about my virtues. He was the most important person in my life while I lived at home. Our codependent relationship is common in dysfunctional families.

I was helpless to relieve his pain because that was something only he could do with the right kind of professional help. I remember my brother as the most frightening person I could ever encounter, but I also remember him as a wonderful, loving brother who gave me more than anyone else could ever have given me when I needed it so desperately.

Many times, he gave me a reason to live by believing in me and believing in my potential. I am thankful for his life and sad that it was filled with pain. I am sad that he had to end it to end the pain. He will always be the most important, caring, loving person in my memory during those difficult childhood years of loss and grief.

My two brothers.

A Lifetime of Losses

My Father's Story

My father died in February 2005. He was ninety-seven years old and still driving his car and living in his own house. I always admired his ability to survive losses and live with determination and vigor.

His father was a violent, abusive man. At one point, he lined up the entire family and was going to shoot them. A neighbor stopped him. When my father was thirteen, his father beat him unconscious and left him lying in a ditch. When he came to, he ran away from home and stayed away for many years.

My mother and father married very young. Both had come from abusive families, and my mother never really had a home. Her mother died when she was two years old. They were both looking for love and acceptance. Unfortunately, their parents never loved them.

My entire family fell apart after the death of my brother. My mother became a drug-dependent, alcoholic, suicidal woman. The problems of my mother and surviving brother added to my father's overwhelming grief. My father felt so impotent as his beloved son suffered from colon cancer.

My mother stayed with her sister in the city while my brother was being treated. My dad worked in the city and would come home on weekends. My father lost one son to cancer, and he was losing his other son to grief.

When my brother was diagnosed with cancer, we did not have life insurance or health insurance. There was no welfare system and no food stamps. The bills piled up. We were impoverished before my brother became terminally ill. We lived in the slums of the city, but when he became ill, my father bought a small farm, which made driving and car costs higher than when we lived in the city.

When my brother died, my father bought six grave plots. My brother was buried in one of them. My father began to drink heavily in the last stages of my brother's death and became a full-blown alcoholic shortly after his death. My mother became addicted to narcotics and alcohol. We lost track of the times she either accidentally or purposely overdosed. It became a way of life.

My father had been born into a family of profound grief. His mother had emigrated from Norway and brought her mother with her. My grandmother's family had four sons and three daughters. In one afternoon, all four sons drowned in a fjord in Norway. It was a terrible loss because male children held primary importance in that family, and all the males who would have provided heirs had died in one day. My great-grandfather also died, and left my great-grandmother and her three daughters. They immigrated to America for a new start.

I traced my family's history back more than 150 years and found losses too profound to grieve. It was carried over from one generation to another. Expressions of grief were not allowed. They thought showing it would mean they were weak. They did not touch or hug because it was a forbidden practice in emotionally constipated families, and this was always hard for me. I desperately needed to be touched. My father finally learned to touch and hug in the last three years of his life. What a shame!

The longer my mother lived, the more mentally ill she became. I do not know how my father was able to keep full-time work and keep up to my mother's medical costs. She ran from one doctor to another so she could get enough narcotics to "feel no pain."

On Mother's Day, she took a huge overdose. My sister and her family had been there and gone home. My brother and his family had been there and gone home. I always attended family affairs after everyone else had gone home to avoid the drinking and obnoxious behavior.

I brought my gift into her bedroom. She was unconscious under a gray wool blanket. I tried to awaken her. I pulled the blanket down and noticed that she had deep burns on one arm. I later learned that she had gotten up in the middle of the night to fix something to eat. She was stoned and fell forward on the hot burner. She had third-degree burns on that arm and burns on both hands.

I told my father we had to get her to a hospital. He refused and said, "She's happy like this." I called my sister to ask for help. She said she would not help me and that we should just let her "die happy."

I threatened my father by telling him that if she died and the police found out how long she had been unconscious, they would charge him with neglect or something more serious. He finally agreed to take her to the hospital. We carried her out to the car and took her to the hospital. They examined her, but they could not keep her because they did not have a bed in lockup. We loaded her back into the car—she was still unconscious—and went home.

I called the doctor who had given her thirty-four prescriptions that she had used to overdose. I explained the emergency to his wife when she answered the phone. She told her husband who was calling and came back to the phone. She said, "I'm sorry, but my husband does not take any calls on Mother's Day." I tried to reason with her, but she hung up on me.

I decided to call a psychiatrist who consulted at the same nursing home/high-rise where I was employed. I apologized to him for bothering him on Mother's Day and asked for his help. He called a hospital/mental health center and made a reservation for my mother. Once again, we loaded her into the car and took her to the hospital.

When she finally became coherent the next

day, she found herself in lockup with a whole lot of mentally ill people. She was furious with me. She knew me well enough to know that I was to blame for the predicament she was in. She just wanted to die, and I had prevented it.

After they moved to Arizona, she overdosed again. A helicopter flew into the intersection down the street from their house. When she was revived, she was furious that they did not let her die.

At one point, she claimed that a religious experience had totally changed her. She was giving up alcohol. When I visited her in Arizona, she was drinking out of a bottle while she was preparing supper. I remarked that I thought she had quit drinking. She told me she did not want my father to drink it because he got too nasty. I asked her why she did not just pour it down the sink. She said, "Oh no. Your father would get too mad at me. He wouldn't care if I drank it, but he would be really angry if I poured it down the drain."

Even if she had given up the alcohol, she would not have given up all of the narcotics. She believed they were "medically necessary." She never got the help she needed to heal the brokenness in her life, and she died a little more each day. My mother died of a broken heart in 1987. Her spirit never healed. I do not know how my father stood by her for so many years.

While my mother was alive, my father was unable to save much money. A great deal of their money was spent on the mental illnesses of my mother and surviving brother. Hospitals, drugs, alcohol, and new doctors would give her more pills to medicate her pain. My father was always financially distressed.

After my mom died in 1987, my dad actually had some enjoyable years and was able to save money. He did some things he enjoyed and no longer had the stress of my mother's mental illness. My father's entire life was touched by loss. He survived my mother by fourteen years. I learned a great deal about him during that time. I was terrified of him when I was a child. I hated his drinking and the resultant behavior. In his last years, I understood that he drank to medicate his pain. I loved him unconditionally, and I am grateful that we had some sane time together in his later years. He even learned to touch and hug and tell me he loved me. That was amazing.

I Was in Prison and You Visited Me

A Sister's Story

Every other weekend, she went through the same routine. She left work on Friday night and drove over to her brother's house to pick up his wife and children. They loaded the children in the car and drove to the state prison in Wisconsin, 350 miles away in the neighboring state. It was a long drive with three tired, stressed-out children on their way to visit their father in prison.

When they arrived in the prison town, they rented a room in a dingy motel and slept for a few hours. Most of the families of the convicts stayed at the same hotel. Cost was an important factor because the breadwinners in those families were locked away. Most could barely afford the gas to get there. They had to rely on family and friends to drive them to that remote town. Some of the families slept in their cars because they did not have the money for a motel room.

The visiting hours on the weekends were limited to two hours on Saturday and two hours on Sunday. That required staying over for two nights. It was a long ride for such a short amount of visitation privileges.

The routine of visiting was always the same. All visitors had to be approved to be on the visitor's list or the mailing list. The families checked in with a picture ID and left their purses in lockers. Fruit and other gifts brought for the prisoners were inspected by the prison officials and given to that prisoner if they passed close scrutiny. Contraband was a continual problem. Visitors proceeded through a metal detector. If the alarm went off, they were asked to empty their pockets. If they still did not pass, a guard of the same sex patted them down.

The heavy metal prison gate swung open, and the visitors walked into a cage-like area. The first door slammed shut. For a few seconds, visitors were locked inside a huge metal cage. Then the second metal door swung open, allowing them to pass into the next section and on to the visitor's room. The bone-chilling clang of the metal doors was a reminder of who was in charge at that prison.

The visiting room had very strict regulations. The prisoners were brought from cells, and the visitors were led in. Regulations dictated that a convict and his visitors could embrace (hug, kiss, or touch) upon arrival. Then they separated and were not allowed to make physical contact during the rest of the visit. To ensure that this rule was not broken, guards stood nearby to "write up" any con that violated the rule.

That con would lose "good" points that could affect his privileges and future visitations. Some guards seemed to enjoy this duty a little too much and seemed to be "looking" for someone to write up.

Sometimes the women would smuggle drugs to their mate in the baby's diaper. Others slipped drugs into their mouths before they entered the visiting room and passed them to the convict while kissing. That small amount of drug provided temporary relief for the recipient. The penalty for smuggling contraband was severe, but the stricter the rules became, the more creative the women became. It was never a question of whether or not they would bring drugs to their mate; it was a question of how would they make the transfer.

The convicts were always strip-searched before they returned to their cells so the drugs could not be hidden on their bodies or in their clothing.

Before they left, the visitors were allowed to embrace their loved ones once again. This was always the most difficult time. Women and children cried, and the men looked on helplessly. Then cons were taken back to their cells, and the visitors went back to the entrance.

The loud clanging of the heavy metal gates on the way out seemed to be even more devastating than on the way in. The sister who had brought her brother's family for a visit felt a sword pierce her heart every time she walked through that cage and heard the gate slam behind her. Physically, her brother was not well. He was put on "the old man's gang" at the prison because he could not do heavy work. Mentally, he was in a constant state of depression and spoke often of self-destruction. Spiritually, he had probably been unconscious for most of his life.

The sister understood that he had committed a crime and was paying the price. She also knew that he had never felt loved or wanted and that the pain he carried often pushed him toward self-destruction. She had always loved him, but that was not enough because he did not love himself or feel the love of others. She would continue to love and support him and his family even though she knew it was not enough reason for him to go on living.

Sometimes the sadness of his life overwhelmed her, and she wondered if God could bring any good out of all of that pain.

The Grief We Inherit

A Century of Losses

When we are born, we inherit many things from our ancestors. Unfortunately, one of the things we inherit is the unresolved grief of our parents and grandparents. We learn to express our feelings or keep our feelings to ourselves. We learn to openly express grief—or we are taught that crying and other expressions of grief and sadness are unacceptable. Quite often, we pass those beliefs down to our children.

I spent most of my life trying to figure out what was wrong with my family. Why was it so self-destructive? Why was there so much pain? Family members medicated their pain with alcohol and drugs. Some killed themselves. Others ended up in prison. Some became mentally ill. We were all self-destructive in one way or another.

When I began to look for answers, I learned how my grandparents and great-grandparents influenced my parents' lives and subsequently my own. Sometimes the information was difficult to find.

No one wanted to talk about the negative parts of our family's history. I persisted because I knew the information was important for my own recovery process.

During my recovery, many people said, "Don't dwell on the past. You must forget the past. Digging up the past accomplishes nothing." To some extent, that is true. We cannot spend our lives painfully reliving the past, regretting the past, or actively blaming the past.

Before we can release the past and let go of the pain, we have to understand something about it. We need to know why the past causes us so much pain and how it continues to impact our lives today. Before we can begin the process of a healthy recovery, we need to go through a process of discovery. Before we can unlearn old, destructive behaviors, we need to know something about how and why we acquired them in the first place.

We need to look honestly at why we believed and practiced self-destructive lifestyles for so long without questioning the validity of our beliefs. In order to do that, we need to look at the history of our ancestors. When we learn about our ancestors, we learn a great deal about ourselves. This can be a very painful process.

We do not look to the past to excuse our own behavior—or anyone else's behavior. We try to understand its impact on our lives. The information may be hard to discover because of family secrets, shame, or death. It is important to find out as much as we can while older family members are still alive.

I want to share some of the discoveries I made in researching my family history. The stories speak for themselves and explain a great deal about my parents and why our family was so self-destructive.

I learned about multiple losses in my father's family and my mother's family. In my mother's family, four of her siblings died of diphtheria in six days. My mother was child number eight, and she was two years old when her mother died as the result of a botched abortion. My mother was then given to a Catholic orphanage because she was considered a burden on her father's farm.

When the losses occurred, there was very little understanding about loss and grief. You simply moved on with your life without spending time on grief. You had to keep a stiff upper lip. There was no time to grieve one loss—let alone four losses. In attempting to retrace my family history, I visited the cemetery where my mother's siblings were buried. I was offended to learn that the children were buried in a mass grave and no longer had headstones on their graves. I realize it was necessary to bury bodies as quickly as possible during a diphtheria epidemic, but it seemed so cold. It helped me understand why my grandmother had so much difficulty grieving the loss of those four children. Her life became self-destructive, and she died while carrying a child that allegedly was not my grandfather's. The pain in her life must have been tremendous.

I have lost only one child, and I suffered unresolved grief and guilt for twenty-two years. I know how the loss of one child affected me, and I cannot imagine what it would be like to lose four children in six days. There was no grieving the children one at a time. Each child had been a unique and special individual, and yet they were buried as one. It is no wonder that my grandmother had difficulty resolving her grief!

I learned that my grandfathers were stern and unsympathetic. They were also abusive and violent. I'm sure they must have grieved, but they masked their grief with violence. They demanded strict adherence to their rules of conduct. There were no tears allowed. Tears were a sign of weakness. There could be no excuse to slow life's usual pace, not even the deaths of several children. They simply buried them in a mass grave and got on with life. The admonition to be strong is still vibrating 135 years later, and I became a victim of that belief.

My mother and father were both physically and emotionally battered children. I wonder how they survived their childhoods. They certainly could not have learned good parenting skills from their parents. When they married and had four children of their own, they had only their own parents as role models. Tragically, they were not positive role models.

My grandmothers were quiet, gentle, and loving women, but they had little influence over violent, volatile men. Women in those times could not defend themselves or their children from the wrath of the men. The men set the rules of conduct and were the disciplinarians in the households. The women were loving and supportive to the children in those private moments that they could get by with it, but those were far too little to compensate for the abuse the men meted out regularly. I'm sure there were times when the women's anger and powerlessness overwhelmed them and they took their feelings out on those smaller and weaker than themselves.

Society did not interfere in the home. A man's home is his castle. Even if outsiders were aware of horrible abuses, they would not have interfered. The law was impotent when it came to matters in the home. It always amazed me that we had a formal organization to protect the rights of animals long before we organized one to protect abused humans.

After learning the details of my mother's childhood, I am convinced that she never had a chance in life. Her mind and spirit were battered from the moment of conception and throughout her entire childhood. She was born to grieve. Even after she left home and married, the circumstances of her life only served to pile up more losses and convince her that she was a terrible person who did not deserve to live.

I journeyed through my ancestry and found alcoholism, drug dependence, suicide, incest, family violence, murder, criminal activities, and so many personal losses that were never grieved. I found entire childhoods that were void of human compassion and the basics of human decency.

I no longer need to question why my family was so dysfunctional. We all inherited more than one lifetime of grief.

I think it would have been difficult to change the beliefs about myself if I had not researched the lives of my ancestors. I needed to understand the years of imprinting that went into making me the person I became. Even though we understand why people did what they did, it does not excuse them. It makes the process of forgiveness a lot easier to work through to completion. It helped me realize that the negative opinions about me were invalid because I am a beautiful, worthwhile person who deserves to live and be loved.

When I speak publicly, I impress upon the audience how important it is for them to research their family histories. It may not be easy, but it is essential for us to understand what has impacted our own lives and made us who we are today.

I speak frequently to high school students about death, dying, and the way children and youth grieve. I also teach about chemical health and chemical dependency. The students have written letters after my visits. I am amazed at the depth of their sharing and how deeply affected they are by the information I share. Some of them have carried grief and low self-worth for most of their lives. As I am speaking, I am aware of their body language and facial expressions. I know I have touched a personal nerve.

Our Spiritual Faith

A Gift or a Curse?

My first book, *Strength for Each Day*, was published in 1986 and reprinted in 1991. It was a daily devotional based on the Twelve Steps of Alcoholics Anonymous and shared religious and spiritual concepts. As I undertake the writing of a new book, I am considering whether or not I should make the emphasis of the book religious. I made that decision for a very important reason.

When I first became a chemical dependency counselor, the large number of people who had given up on their religious beliefs and lost their faith in God surprised me. Some felt that they had personally failed God too many times and could not be forgiven by him. Others felt that God had disappointed them too often. If He was a loving God, He would have been there when they needed Him most. Some had no religious training in their homes as children and had no understanding of faith in God. Many believed in a Higher Power, but that Higher Power was not God. Many belief systems do not choose our God as their God.

I have experienced many positive and negative feelings about faith and God. At some times, my faith became my strength and helped me maintain my balance. It helped me maintain my sanity during times that were so stressful that I might have killed myself. For a great part of my life, my faith has been a genuine gift.

As the losses piled up in my life, I did not have time to grieve one before another one hit. My physical health and emotional health were stretched to the limit and exhausted my spiritual health. I lost sight of my faith, but I reached the point where I did not believe there could possibly be a God. I rationalized that even if there *might* be a God, He either did not care about me or did not know I existed. What good was He?

When I was going through those desert experiences, my faith was definitely a curse. In fact, I felt guilty about losing my faith in God. My faith experience added another burden to an already overburdened human spirit. I have cursed God, denied God, called Him a "turkey," and told Him in no uncertain terms that He was useless. I have tried to bargain with God and demanded that He take some of my burdens down the street to another doorstep. I have accused Him of underestimating my coping ability. I have shouted many times, "Why me, God? Why me?" The only answer to that question I ever received was, "Why not me? And if not me, then who?" Frankly, there was never anyone else I would have wished that many trials on.

One personal experience made it impossible to deny God's existence. I was very depressed because of my family and my health. I decided to go for a walk and took my camera with me. There was no sun, and it was raining off and on. I decided to take pictures of the gloomy day since it represented the way I felt. I said, "I don't believe you exist! I can't see you. I can't hear you. I can't feel you. You do not seem to care about me. If you do exist, you will have to prove it me. Give me some kind of a sign. You had better hit me over the head with a very large board because I really can't sense your presence." I snapped several pictures and returned to my cabin.

Three weeks later, I got the pictures back. One of my kids said, "Mom, how did you manage to get this picture?" I looked at the picture to see what they were talking about and got goose bumps. The dark, gray clouds were in the sky, but in the middle of the dark clouds, there was a bright light in the perfect shape of a cross. All around the cross, there was a bright circle of light. I keep an enlargement on my wall and share it with others when I speak in churches. I had demanded that He show me a sign, and He had given me a sign I could not deny. I did not expect any answer, but that answer was so profound that I could never again deny His existence.

I have also seen religion and Christianity used as a way to control, manipulate, and abuse other people. I have had so-called Christians interpret the Bible out of context and use it to shame me. I have been disenchanted with the fellowship of Christian believers. During those times, I need to remind myself that they are imperfect humans like myself. I need to be tolerant of them without allowing them to abuse me. It is unfortunate that these people can do more harm than good to the cause of Christianity.

My Christian faith is more of a gift than a curse. Since I know how discouraged we can get during difficult times, I do not presume to think that all people feel that way. I have included this chapter on spiritual faith, but I did not make the emphasis of the book spiritual or religious.

There might be information in this book that would be helpful to some hurting people. If they are angry with God or have given up on Him, they would not read a book that was totally religious. I felt it was important to share my personal beliefs in one chapter without forcing it on those who are not interested.

Abortion and Adoption

The Other Child Losses

There are other childhood losses that set us up for profound grief. Abortion or adoption may seem like the only solution at the time, but they leave us with a special kind of grief.

There are many reasons why a decision is made to abort a fetus. An unwed mother may decide it is too difficult to raise a child alone. A family may have too many children, and another child would create a crisis in the marriage and family. The couple may not have even wanted children. Perhaps a mother knows her mate would seriously abuse the baby. The fetus may have serious deformities or health problems. The girl/woman may have been raped. Whether the reason is right or wrong for the individual person is not important. Most women struggle a great deal before reaching the decision to abort. Dealing with the aftermath of an abortion is not easy.

The women I know whom had abortions suffered a great deal before reaching the decision. All were aware that it was a human life. All felt desperate and felt is was necessary for them. They suffered terrible guilt before, during, and after the abortion. Most carried that guilt for many years. One woman was never able to get pregnant again and felt it was punishment for the abortion. She spent a great deal of time feeling guilty and grieving the child she had aborted.

In my mother's case, she aborted two babies to save her marriage. The financial stress during the Depression with four small children and my father unemployed was just too difficult to deal with. She carried that grief to the grave. She hated my father for forcing her to have the abortions. My parents had three children in less than four years. My father told my mother that if she got pregnant one more time, he would leave her and the children. The problem was that he was a very sexual young man and demanded sex frequently. There was no birth control in the 1930s.

My grandmother died as a result of an abortion. She was forty-six years old when my mother was born. She was forty-seven when she had another miscarriage and forty-eight when she died from a botched abortion. She never fully recovered from losing for children to diphtheria in one week. An elderly aunt told me that neither of the last two babies were my grandfather's. She was allegedly having an affair with a live-in farmhand. My aunt said it was questionable whether my mother was my grandfather's child. With all the unresolved grief, I could see why she attempted to abort her last baby. It cost her life and left my mother an orphan.

In the 1990s, abortion was very controversial, but desperate women have done it for hundreds of years. It wasn't very safe, but it was a regularly practiced solution for unwanted pregnancies. The couple was very sexual, but there was no surefire method of birth control. Total abstinence caused other problems in the marriage. You only had to have sex once every nine months, and the consequences could be a child to raise for eighteen or more years. Many did not want more children and could not afford them.

During the 1930s, a woman simply paid fifty dollars to have a man come to the house and perform an abortion. That was a lot of money during those difficult times, but it was not as costly as raising a child.

My best friend used an even more frightening method to abort her unwanted babies. She simply straightened a wire coat hanger and shoved it up until she started to hemorrhage. That was pretty dangerous, and she nearly died on one occasion. For many women, the consequences of having another baby were higher than the risks of an abortion. Desperate women do desperate things, even at the cost of their lives.

There was no counseling available back then. Women made the decision and tried to live with it. Although counseling is available to many women today, it is probably only required or available in the better clinics. A safe abortion can be more costly than a self-administered one. Some women take what they think is the least expensive and least public way to abort. That decision can be very costly in the long run, but they do not consider the serious consequences at that point. Other women are forced into a decision to abort by family members and never agree with the decision, even though they may go through with it. Their grief can become very profound because they believe they should have done something to stop the abortion, even though they may have been powerless at the time to do anything.

The decision to give up a child for adoption brings another set of circumstances. It can bring difficult, prolonged grief. The women I know who have given up a child for adoption say that they look for that child's face everywhere they go. *Could that be my child?*

The decision to give up a child is made for many reasons. Some women make the decision, and at other times, family members or society pressure them into it. If the woman/girl does not want to give up the child, but agrees because of pressure or shame, and the guilt is even more profound. She will carry anger or hatred toward those who pressured her into it as well as toward herself for giving in.

One Rose

My mother pulled me by the arm to the casket at the front of the church. I resisted and she squeezed my arm tightly and placed my hand on the body. She spoke very sternly. "Say goodbye to Buddy." My fifteen-year-old brother had died of cancer. He had been sick for three years.

This body in the coffin weighed only fifty pounds. His hair was snow white. His eyes were sunken back in his head. His cheeks had fallen so far they had carved huge caverns in his face. His fingers were bones barely covered with skin and they were icy cold.

They said he was dead. I did not believe it. Everyone had said he would get well and come home. My dad bought six grave plots. I thought that meant that more of us were going to die. No one talked about what happened except to say, "don't talk about it, it makes your mother sad."

I was eleven years old and too scared to ask, too scared to use that word, "die." It was such a scary word, a sad word, and a final word.

My sister was sixteen and my brother was thirteen;

they were old enough to visit our brother in the city hospital. I was eleven, and the hospital rules said I was too young to visit. I had not seen him for more than a year and a half when he died.

We lived on a farm near a small town. My dad worked in the city and came home on weekends. My mom stayed in the city to be near my brother. As he became sicker, she stayed away longer.

It wasn't that I did not ask. I had asked a lot of people if my brother would get well and come home. The well-meaning people from the big church in town said, "God can make him well. You just need to pray for him." So I prayed for him to get well.

When my parents were in the city with my brother, my siblings took care of me. They weren't nice to me. They would lock me in the dirt cellar beneath the kitchen floor and put the table on top. There were no lights, no windows and lots of creepy, crawly creatures. At first I was terrified. Sometimes they tied me to a chair and fed me food I hated.

I decided it was nicer in the cellar than it was upstairs with them. At eight, I learned that I was powerless to change things in my life. My sister and brother were stronger than I was. The first couple of times I was locked up, I was terrified. Then from the desperation born out of fear, I made friends with the darkness. I made friends with the crawling creatures that shared my dark, damp hole.

I knew I could not continue to get that scared every time they locked me up. When I got scared, they seemed to enjoy it. I could not let them win. I could not let them conquer me. My body was locked up, but my spirit was free. I wrote poems in my mind and put them down on paper later in my room. They were my secret thoughts about fear, anger, loneliness, and death. I would not share them with anyone!

If I got really nasty and threatened them, they would leave me down there even longer. When I thought they were going to let me out, I screamed through the floor at them. I shouted insults and threats that made them furious. To punish me, they left me there longer, which was just what I wanted. I won by letting them think they were in control.

While Buddy was getting sicker, my parents were fighting more. They were drinking a lot on the weekends. The family was falling apart, and no one talked about it.

Life was awful. Every time my brother and sister came home, they were very quiet. They were mean. My mom was sad all the time, and she cried a lot. My dad drank a lot, but he hardly talked anymore. I knew something bad was happening, but no one said anything. No one told me my brother would die!

I needed my mother to be home with me! One night, I shouted, "God, if he's not going to get better and come home soon, I wish he would just hurry up and die." When he died three weeks later, I thought I had killed him. Didn't God know that I did not mean what I said? I felt so guilty. How could I ever look my mother in the eyes again? What if she knew

I had told God that I wanted him dead? She would hate me for the rest of my life. She was already so broken. I hoped she would never learn that I had killed him.

The funeral was awful. When my brother left the farm, he looked good. He weighed about a hundred pounds. His hair was light brown and curly. I saw him only a few times during the early part of his illness. He did not look terrible. He was thin and sickly, but he still looked like my brother. He had a colostomy. I thought that was gross.

As my hand touched his hands, I started to shake. It was like touching an electric fence with wet hands. Someone removed me from the coffin, and I held to the rose I had grabbed from his lapel. The rose was the only real thing about that day.

The adults changed their stories. They said things like, "God needed another angel in heaven" and "God needed your brother in Heaven more than here on Earth." Some even said he was better off dead. Grownups could not be trusted or believed. I decided there was no God. If there was a God, he was a terrible, cruel God, and I wanted nothing to do with Him. He could not be trusted either.

I never believed that Buddy was in that coffin. All my memories of my brother left when I touched his hand, but I would always have that one rose. The rose was all I had left, except for grief. That scary face haunted me for many years.

I still have the rose pressed in my Bible. Even

though sixty-four years have passed, I remember that day like it was yesterday. I have no memories of the childhood we shared, but I will always remember that I had wished him dead.

Failure To Bond

Neglect and Abuse

When a child suffers from failure to bond as a result of poor physical or emotional health of the mother and or father, little can be done to correct the situation. Parents can be overwhelmed by the costs of care and consequences of an ill mother. If there is a father present, he cannot fill both roles for the child.

Failure to bond because of neglect or abuse is even more difficult to change. Not all women who become pregnant want to have babies or even care about a new life. In some cases, neither parent wants a child. The child exists only because of unprotected sex. That is really sad.

The child is born with no support system. There may be no physical holding other than feeding and changing. In some cases, even those simple requirements are not met.

When my children were young, I was a Brownie leader for the Girl Scouts. Although I lived more than a block away from a little girl in my troop, her neighbors called me to ask for help with those children. I was the only one who dared to call for help.

It was thirty degrees below zero when I received more calls for those children. The oldest child went to try to get help. She walked barefoot to a neighbor's house with no coat, no boots, and short pajamas. I reluctantly got involved because it seemed useless to call the local child protection services. I had tried before with no results.

In the middle of the night, I went over to the little girl's house. She had four younger siblings, and the youngest was ten months old. What I found was shocking. A wood stove heated their old cement house. The five children all slept on a mattress on the floor with one scanty blanket. The house was cold and drafty.

The children were hungry. I checked the cupboards and refrigerator, but they were empty except for beer and booze. There was no milk or formula for the baby.

I went into the baby's room and was shocked to find an undernourished baby. There were dirty baby clothes and dirty bedding all over the room. The smell was putrid. The baby was too weak to even roll over in his crib. He was on a bare plastic mattress and had sores all over his body and scalp. His cry was weak and pitiful.

My own baby was ten months old, and the comparison between the two was frightening. I stayed there until the mother came home the next day. She explained that the children were fine by themselves and asked me to leave.

I called child protective services and asked them to check into the situation. I was "scolded" for sticking my nose in someone else's business and pretty much told off.

The next week, I got a call that the children were alone again in a cold house. I called child protective services, and they declined to become involved. I threatened them by saying that if anything happened to those children, the first phone call I would make would be to the newspaper. I told them that if a fire started and the house burned with the children in it, the entire community would know they had been contacted and failed to respond. There were cigarettes, lighters, and matches all over the house.

They were forced to intervene. They told the mother what she would have to do to keep her children and took all of them to a doctor. The mother moved them out of town in the middle of the night with no forwarding address. The children would not receive the help they needed and deserved. The house was condemned and torn down. The children and mother were never found.

This is a simple example of how much some children suffer in the care of their parents. These children had no father, and their mother was totally irresponsible. She was more interested in her own pleasure than in the needs of her children. The children were on their own, and the oldest child was responsible for all of her siblings. What a terrible position to be in at a time when the children should have been involved in being children.

We became foster parents because we wanted to add a little boy to our household. We had a son, three biological daughters, and one teen foster daughter. The county offered us a seven-year-old boy, but he came with a nine-year-old sister. We agreed to take them both.

The children needed foster care because an older sister had been in an asthmatic hospital in Denver. The parents drove down to pick her up and bring her home. On the way home, they stopped to celebrate her birthday. The parents had liquor for that celebration. They were intoxicated. As the father attempted to pass a truck loaded with hogs, he miscalculated and hit the truck. His wife was decapitated, and his daughter was seriously injured. She was not wearing her medical identification bracelet when she arrived at the hospital. They were unaware of her serious medical problems. She also died.

The father was sentenced to eighteen months in prison. The children moved in with an uncle, but he died. Then they moved in with a grandmother, and she became seriously ill. Everyone around them was dead or too sick to care for them. The children spoke freely of the tragedies in their lives. They made a lot of people very uncomfortable. They would say, "My mom's head was cut right off." They would talk about all the people who had died. I was frequently asked if I was scared about taking in the two children because everyone around them seemed to die.

The little boy was especially needy. He would sit on my lap, lean his head against my chest, and stroke my breasts as if to reassure him that comfort was close. That made a lot of people uncomfortable in the 1970s, but I understood that he was thinking of his mother. He needed that reassurance.

I took the children to visit their father in prison twice a month. Those visits were difficult for the children and the father. They had grown up around drinking behavior, but they did not understand the severe consequences of drinking until they visited their father in prison. They experienced so many losses in such a short period of time that there was not enough time to grieve all the losses. They were thrown into an entirely new environment with new rules and strange people.

Children are often taken out of really bad situations and dumped into totally strange environments. All of the children we eventually took into our homes had significant problems and needed professional help. Some were victims of incest or other forms of violence. Some had lost family members or were abandoned.

When I would ask for help for the children, I was told that there was a long waiting list for professional counseling. I was told to wait. Most of them never got the help they needed.

Our Children's Teachers

The Good, the Bad, the Damaging

I have been aware since early childhood how teachers can make a huge difference in the lives of children who have a lot of grief, losses, or trauma. Unfortunately, teachers are just like the rest of the population. There are excellent, caring, sensitive teachers who can make the difference between success and failure, and high self-worth and low self-worth in children who are hurting deeply. There are also some very scary, destructive teachers who bring hurting children to the edge of the abyss and then push them over.

Some teachers have not resolved their own childhood grief/loss issues. Some are still unhappy in their adult lives, and their students are affected by their unresolved conflicts. Others have health problems, are going through divorces, or are taking care of aging parents.

It is irrelevant whether you are a police officer, a doctor, a counselor, or a teacher. If you are in helping profession and are still carrying unresolved issues that damage your life, it will affect those you are charged with helping. Some of the scariest teachers I have encountered are those who were raised by perfectionist parents. They have the same demands for their students. These teachers were especially damaging to the children we had in foster care who were victims of incest and other forms of violence.

My entire childhood was impacted by the fact that I was an unwanted child and was reminded of that almost every day. No matter how hard I tried, I was never good enough or smart enough to win my mother's love or acceptance. There was not a single adult in my life that was able to find any purpose for my being. I constantly drew criticism and scorn.

After my brother died, I got into trouble in school and ended up in detention for nearly three school years of high school. I had two teachers who were responsible for supervising me in detention. My algebra teacher called me aside and let me know how much I was inconveniencing him. He said, "Vetsch, I would rather go home and spend time with my family rather than stay in detention with you all the time." He was right, of course, but I could have cared less about his problems.

My chemistry teacher called me aside one night and said, "Vetsch, I can't understand why you keep getting into so much trouble. You are so intelligent, and you have so much you could offer this world! You can accomplish anything you decide to do once you make up your mind."

That was the first time a grown-up had told me

my life had value and that I was smart. That message went straight to my heart, and although I did not change immediately, I started to believe what he told me. I had always been on the honor roll, and I always received D's and F's in conduct. My teachers filled all the white spaces on my report cards with critical remarks. No one realized that I was in a profound state of grief. I was kicked out of home economics on three different occasions. Later in life, I realized that my home economics teacher was too much like my mother. I resented that. I did not want to be like my mother!

The caption under my senior picture in the yearbook was "The Blonde Bombshell," but it wasn't because I was a peroxided blonde. It was because I was a bombshell waiting to go off without warning. The captain of the football team was harassing me one day, and I decked him, giving him a huge black eye. The nickname was also given to me by the boys because I was really stacked and had large breasts.

That chemistry teacher saved my life and was partially responsible for many of the tasks I have taken on and succeeded at. The tiniest ray of hope for a wounded child can keep him or her going in the right direction.

My son had a very destructive male teacher in the fourth grade. I eventually got to know him well enough to recognize that he was carrying a lot of garbage from his own childhood and school days. My son was a daydreamer. He would look out the window, and that would drive this teacher crazy. The teacher was a control freak, and the issue became a power struggle between the two of them. He treated my son the same way his father must have treated him—with emotional, verbal, and physical force to bring him into compliance with his own rules. That did not work with my son.

The teacher called me in for a special conference. When I arrived, he said, "I have decided that your son is *profoundly* retarded and that he will never be able to do any better than he is doing now, which is not very well!"

At the time, I was not as well informed as I am today and did not know the true meaning of the words "profoundly retarded." I agreed to have him tested by the school district, and the results were the same as his previous years. He was at grade level in some things and above grade level in others.

That teacher did so much damage to my son's belief in his own ability that it followed him throughout school and beyond. He did not even attempt to go beyond high school. At the age of fifty-five, he still remembers the impact of that teacher on his life. He had been given "dummy" messages that he was unable to move beyond.

On the first day of junior high school, he was whispering with a friend. His shop teacher picked him up off the stool *by his hair* and kicked him so hard that he left a permanent footprint on my son's new pants. When I confronted the teacher and the principal the next day, he said, "I have to establish discipline, starting with the first day, and your son was whispering!" I informed the teacher that what he called *discipline* was what the human rights organization that I had contacted called *child abuse*. I informed him that he would pay me for a new pair of pants and apologize to my son. He did.

I also informed him that if he had done that to my foster son, he could have put him in a wheelchair for life because of his disability. He told me not to worry because if it had been my foster son, his records would have been flagged. He would have known that he could not be physical with him. That was no comfort to me. I said, "So what you are telling me is that you know which children you can physically abuse and which ones you can't abuse?" He did not reply, but he understood fully that he'd better not abuse *any* of my children.

After that incident, I became involved in children's rights organizations and was appointed to a nine-county children's rights legislative committee to help draft legislation for children's rights.

I think that all teachers should be required to read *A Child Called It!* If teachers need convincing that human decency pays off in the classroom, this book should convince them. Another excellent book is *Toxic Parents*, which explains the devastation to the human spirit brought about by sick and dysfunctional parents.

I know all of the arguments:

1. There are too many troubled children to deal with in the schools today.

2. Budget cuts have cut teachers, paraprofessionals, etc.
3. Class size has increased, workload has increased, and help has decreased.
4. There is too much to do in a day now, and teachers have no more to give.

That's all true! If we can keep an open heart and an open mind when dealing with children who somehow provoke us, perhaps we might be the only rays of hope in a very dark world. I hope so. If we cannot help these children, at the very least, we must not add to their daily burdens. I survived a destructive childhood because a teacher saw something positive in spite of all of my problems and gave me hope. I will be forever grateful for that teacher!

If we do not reach and touch the hurting children of today, they will become the incarcerated adults of tomorrow. America will pay dearly for our lack of caring. Even if we do not help for the noblest reason of all, human decency, we should do it for selfish reasons so that our children and grandchildren can live in a peaceful and safe world.

A Miracle in the Desert!

It had not rained for a very long time in Arizona. As the old woman walked through the arid desert, she wondered how plants and creatures could survive in a desert that had been dry for so long. Even the cactuses that usually thrived looked as if they were struggling in the heat. Bushes and other vegetation that had given the desert a tint of green looked brown and shriveled. The ground seemed to reflect the heat so intensely that it became almost suffocating.

The little creatures that usually scurried around the desert must have crawled into burrows to protect themselves from the intense heat. Even the desert wrens were hidden from view in the heat of the day. The lizards that rushed from bush to bush for protection were noticeably absent.

There were few signs of life as the old woman strolled through the desert. She paused for a moment to wonder why she had ventured into the desert on such a stifling day. She regretted her decision to go for a walk in the desert because the heat was so intense. Her body was drenched in perspiration, and it was difficult to breathe.

She was about to turn around and go home when she saw an amazing sight in front of her. She saw a lily in full bloom. Its leaves were bright green, and it had several blossoms that seemed to reach for the sun. Everything around it was brown and crisp. It seemed impossible for a lily with such breathtaking beauty to be so vibrant and lush. The lily stood out like a trumpet in the silence of midnight.

The old woman knew that lilies did not grow naturally in the desert. She knew that nature had created a miracle. Wild birds ate the seeds of the lilies in people's yards and dropped the seeds in the desert. The seeds germinated and grew into beautiful plants, even though there was little rain to nourish them.

As the old woman bent over to look at this miracle, she noticed that the lily had only a thin, delicate root that was partially sticking out of the ground. The ground around the lily was parched and cracked like the lines on a map. She was amazed as she examined the tiny root that supported such a magnificent flower.

The old woman paused to contemplate the meaning of the day. She was reminded of the delicate balance in her own life. There had been times when her life seemed dead and malnourished. She seemed unable to find sustenance to keep going during times of loss. Just dying out like the vegetation in the desert seemed to be her only hope for relief. She struggled to keep going, even though there seemed to be no way to refresh her wounded spirit. She longed for something, anything, to renew the vitality she had once felt. She prayed to a God even though she doubted His existence. There was only deafening silence like the silence in the desert.

She was reminded of the strength of the huge saguaro cactus. The cactus often seemed dry and lifeless. It was filled with perhaps a ton of water that sustained it from one rain until another. In the spring, the cactus breaks forth with a beautiful display of flowers. The blooming cactuses in the desert are one more example of a miracle in the desert.

The old woman was reminded that, even when her life was at its lowest point, a supply of nourishment always remained deep within her soul. It would sustain her through arid times. She needed to believe that she could find that tiny seed of faith that would revive her spirit as it had for many years.

The miracle in the desert renewed her hope. There was a purpose, after all, for her walk in the desert that day. As long as she had life, she had hope. The miracle in the desert had reminded her to bloom where she was planted.

When a Mother's Grief Turns Inward

When an infant or a child dies, a mother's life is turned upside down. The same is true if a child is born with a disability or a serious health problem. The mother will take full responsibility for her child's death or health problem. The cause of the child's death or health problem does not matter. She convinces herself it is her fault. She may turn against others, but the focus of her guilt and blame is herself. Some of that guilt has been given to her because of the history of grief in her family. Our families teach us to grieve in healthy ways or a destructive ways.

When a child dies or is diagnosed with a serious health problem, many people send the wrong kind of messages. Instead of comforting or supporting the mother, they dump their own beliefs on her. They are sharing their own grief history. Unfortunately, that includes the medical professionals and spiritual counselors who should be helping us.

A mother can punish herself in many ways when harm comes to her child.

1. God must be angry with her!
2. She was not dedicated enough to God and Christ.
3. She did not love her child enough.
4. She did not want the baby badly enough.
5. She is a very bad mother.
6. She did not take good enough care of herself when she was pregnant.
7. She "should have known something was wrong."
8. Her husband did not love her and the baby enough.
9. If she recommits her life to Christ, she will be forgiven, and her other children will be safe from harm.

Many people are willing to believe that God was disappointed or angry with them and that their children have paid the price for their sins. If other people say that, it does not help anyone.

When my second daughter was three years old, she was diagnosed with a brain tumor. We were given a very dismal outlook for her life. In the 1950s, there were multiple specialists available to complete the diagnosis. We had to wait three weeks to see the pediatric specialist. My husband did not attend church at all.

One of the ladies from my church pulled me aside after the service and said, "Vetsch, are you willing to pay the price of your daughter's life for your husband's salvation?"

I asked her what in the world she meant.

She said, "Your daughter is probably going to die because your husband is not saved. God is punishing both of you for his refusal to be saved and turn his life over to Christ."

I looked her straight in the face and replied, "First of all, I do not believe that God would allow a child to suffer so terribly because He was angry at the parents. Secondly, the only way I can continue to believe in God is because I believe He is a loving God who wants the best for His children and grandchildren. I absolutely cannot believe in a cruel, vengeful God who kills children to teach their parents a lesson in obedience. Perhaps just as important, there is no guarantee that my husband will be saved if our little daughter dies. He may become so angry and hurt that he turns away from God forever."

She resented my defense, but I could not allow her poison to infect my grief process. The struggle was hard enough already.

I counseled numerous people who had turned away from God because of tragedies in their lives. We need to remember that we do not have control over many areas in our lives. We cannot blame God and should not blame ourselves for the areas of our lives we do not control.

I was introduced to this Christian belief that God is getting even with you at the tender age of eight. Once again, the so-called Christians gave me advice about why my brother was dying. These adults assured me my brother would get well under certain conditions. That meant we had a choice, and we had control over his life and death. I never believed he would die.

They said, "God is angry with your mom and dad. Your dad does not go to church and is not saved. Pray for your brother every day, and God will save his life." As I watched my brother suffering and my family falling apart, I prayed several times a day. Those people were wrong! He died, and my family fell apart right in front of my eyes. After he died, those fine folks had reasons for his death.

They said, "God needs your brother in heaven so he will take him to heaven." Boy, that one really sounded stupid. Between the financial devastation and the grief, no one needed my brother more than my family. We did not have health or life insurance and went without many essentials as the disease took over.

They said, "God only loaned him to your parents for a little while. It's time for him to go home with God."

They said, "Your parents will be so much stronger when this is all over. Your dad will be saved, and God will love him again." They did not know my father very well. You just can't threaten a stubborn German. My father refused to believe in God or have anything to do with church or religion from 1947 until he died in 2005 at the age of ninety-seven. God was not a comforter for my father.

We never talked about my brother's death, and we never discussed the impact on our family. At the age of eleven, I crawled inside of myself. The only person I could trust was myself! I became the family caretaker and spent most of my life trying to rescue them. It was heartbreaking. They are all dead now, but their lives were destroyed by unresolved grief.

Perhaps the saddest thing that happens when a mother turns her grief inward is the destructive affect it has on the husband/mate and children. She decides that she married the wrong man or he no longer meets her needs. The husband is confused by her uncaring or hostile attitude. She may withdraw physically and emotionally. She may go on her own spiritual journey and exclude her husband entirely, other than reminding him that he no longer meets her needs. He is also grieving, but his grief is different because of his gender and role in the family.

If a child dies, the grief may not end for the mother. If the child has a serious health problem or severe disability, the mother may focus on that child to the detriment of her husband and other children. The other children's lives may be negatively impacted because of the mother's commitment to one ill child.

When my brother died, my mother's grief became destructive for everyone in our family. She blamed my dad because he told her he would leave if she got pregnant again. It was during the Great Depression, and he was earning a meager income. My mother had only completed third grade because of abuse and neglect in her own home. She was too ill and too frail to attend public school. She could not support herself and the children on her own. She resolved that fear by aborting (or attempting to abort) every pregnancy after the birth of her third child. That left her with impossible guilt and grief. My parents blamed me for all the conflict in the household.

It is important to realize how profoundly a mother's guilt and blame can impact the entire family. She does not just destroy her own chances for happiness. She destroys the opportunity for happiness for her remaining children and spouse.

My sister-in-law would call me when my brother was stoned. He would play Russian roulette with his gun or had slashed his wrists. I would arrive at the house, and he would say, "Vetsch, the folks won't be happy until I am dead. I should have died instead of Buddy! I owe them that much." His only son spent most of his life incarcerated and went to prison for murder a few months after my brother killed himself.

My parents never divorced. They lived together for the remainder of my mother's life. I'm not sure they could have done anything differently. They were both too needy. The unresolved grief profoundly affected our family for generations. What a waste of some beautiful lives!

I cannot say if divorce is wrong or right under difficult circumstances. I divorced after twenty-seven years. The mugging resulted in an ugly disease. My husband could not touch me and was hardly ever home. I considered ending my life, and I filed for divorce. I had known him since I was ten years old.

Filing for divorce was horrible. There had never been a divorce in my entire family. My mother told me that a woman stays with a man "no matter how he treats her." She said, "Even if he beats you and your children, it is a sin to get a divorce." She let me know I was stuck for life, regardless of what occurred in our marriage. When I decided to end my life to stop the pain of neglect, I knew that that divorce was my only choice. I suffered for many years for making that decision. I worried excessively about how God would ever forgive me. I assumed I would go to hell!

It is not wise to stay together for the sake of the children unless couples are going to get the professional help they need. We destroy our children's chances at emotional, mental, and spiritual well-being when we live broken lives in front of them.

It may be financially better to stay together, but that is not a good enough reason. If we can learn to love and respect each other again and resolve the brokenness in our lives, we will come out better. Our children will be healthier. There is no magic person waiting to fill our lives with peace and joy. Work with what you have and get the help you need.

There is one exception to staying together. If one spouse is physically or emotionally abusive, the abused spouse and children must get out before any more damage is done.

Certainly, I understand turning to religion for solace. I did when I was told I was dying after the mugging incident at work. It is destructive if we turn away from our spouses or children and crawl inside our grief. If we abandon everything we believed in before and abandon those who love us because of changed values, we set ourselves up for more loss and grief.

God does not expect us to be perfect. He loves us unconditionally. He forgives us unconditionally. When we convince ourselves that God is punishing us by wounding our children, we dishonor God and His love for us. We ignore his invitation: "Come unto me all ye who are weary and heavy laden and I will give you rest." God also expects us to help ourselves. He does not approve when we sit upon our own pity pot and wait for Him to zap us with healing.

God does not zap us with healing from the tragic losses in our lives. God will not give us amnesia from painful memories and losses. He will encourage us to begin the healing process by working with Him and others. He expects us to work at grief recovery so that we can be the best we can be.

We need to get up off that pity pot and get the help we need. We need to go forward in life as wounded healers and help others who are suffering. We need to mend the broken relationships that resulted from the loss.

The Dirt Cellar

A Place of Hope

The cellar I was locked in was accessed through a hole in the kitchen floor with a trapdoor. A ladder was dropped down, and a light on a long cord was also dropped down. In the beginning, the space was used for storing vegetables we had grown during the summer. When we upgraded to running water, that space held the motor for the pump.

The cellar was damp and cold. There was no flooring and no windows. When my siblings put me in the cellar, I was not allowed the luxury of a light. There was no escape. After several occasions in the cellar I hid a piece of plastic and an old jacket behind the canned goods. That gave me the option of putting on a jacket and sitting on plastic rather than the damp, cold dirt. I probably would have hidden a flashlight, but that was a luxury I did not have. I think I own fifteen or more flashlights now. This seems to be a leftover behavior from the trauma. My siblings would not have allowed me to take a flashlight even if I had one.

As my brother became sicker, the lockups became more frequent. At first, I was so terrified that I thought I would die, and the more upset I got, the more my siblings seemed to enjoy it. On that first occasion I realized I was alone in the dark with creepy, crawly spiders and salamanders. That frightened me more than the darkness. I did not know when one of these creatures was about to crawl on my hands or face. I could not push them away before they crawled on me, because I could not see them coming.

After a few days of terror, I decided I needed to somehow make friends with the darkness, the spiders, and the salamanders. Even at the age of eight, my survival instincts guided me through the ordeal. I had to learn how to get through that terror. I decided it was much nicer in the cellar with my new friends than it was upstairs with my two siblings.

About the time I thought they were going to let me out I would shout insults and threats through the floorboard. I became pretty nasty with my verbal assault. They would leave me down there much longer and that was okay with me. When they finally let me out I would go to the hayloft in the barn and write down my thoughts on death, dying, loneliness, and fear. I believe that was the point in my life that I began to write a book about loss and loneliness. It was also at that point in my life that I began to ponder the meaning of sibling grief and child loss. Even as a young child, my mind was always spinning with questions that I needed answers for to heal my woundedness. The questions led me to some of my educational choices, volunteer choices, and career choices. Although most of my questions have been resolved through research and personal experience, I still wonder why certain things happened the way they did.

My experiences with loss led me to my involvement with foster care. For eight years, we provided licensed foster care for abused children. They felt the same confusion and lack of self-love and self-worth that I had struggled with.

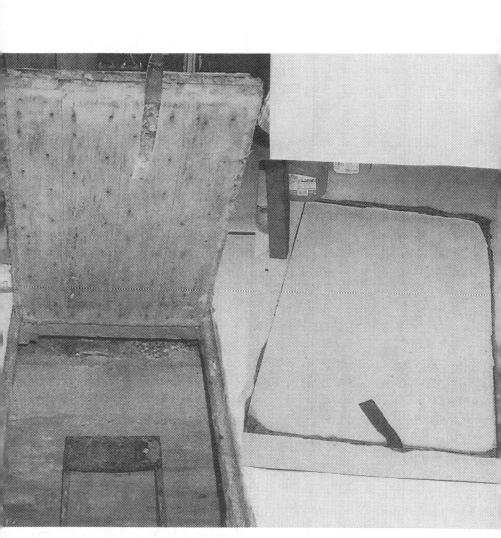

Two photos side by side of the door
into my underground cellar.

Unleashed

I remember the dark, cold cellar
I remember the smell of the musty, wet dirt
I remember the total darkness with no windows
I remember the hole in the ground with no escape
I remember the creepy, crawling creatures
That crawled across my hands and face
I remember the terror of being alone-
I remember the taunting of my captors-
I hated them—my two siblings
I remember making the decision-
To make friends with the darkness
With the darkness in my life
I remember naming each of my creature friends
I remember poems and stories in my head
I remember the decision to survive-
And defeat my captors
They would *not* win!
I remember the cellar made me strong and
    determined
I remember I was eight years old.
They pulled up the ladder to the cellar—
No way to escape

There was no place to sit
I remember I was thirsty
I remember peeing in the corner
I remember shouting and cursing
I threatened them with tattling
I begged them to let me out
When they finally let me out, I went to my room
And wrote down my thoughts and fears
I had to plan ahead to protect myself
I hid a piece of canvas to sit or lay on
And hid it behind the canned goods
I hid toilet paper and an empty bucket
In the cellar so I had a place to pee
I remember the cellar becoming my friend
Away from the torment of my siblings

Silent Cries

No one heard my cries. They were silent cries for help. I was not allowed to cry out loud. I had been programmed at the age of nine to " be strong!" I felt like I was screaming on the inside. The sound could not get out. The sound of crying was the only aspect of my grief that did not get out. My behavior should have alerted someone that I was in trouble, but in 1947, little was known about sibling grief.

My mother's grief took center stage. Her grief was so profound that it consumed all the time and energy of everyone around her. We tiptoed around her so that we wouldn't disturb the delicate balance between sanity and insanity. One wrong move or word could have pushed her over the edge into the dark abyss of madness. I worried about her most of the time. I wondered what would happen to me if she died or killed herself. Who would take care of me if she became insane and had to be locked up?

My mother and I were home alone during the week. I took personal responsibility for her happiness and stability. That was impossible for a child my age, but I had to do my best. Her grief seemed to become more intense as time went on.

My brother kept getting into trouble. My dad would clear up one mess, and my brother would get into trouble again. He was drinking a lot. It hurt me deeply to see my brother so wounded. I was too young to understand why he was so troubled, but I defended him boldly. That usually alienated me from my mother—after another lecture about my sainted dead brother.

My grief came out in inappropriate ways that got me into trouble at school. The teachers said, "Vetsch has an indifferent attitude! Vetsch is very smart, but she seems distracted!" My journalism teacher noted that I was very talented, but I seemed to have a lot on my mind, which interfered with my concentration.

I was considered the class clown. I managed to keep people laughing even though I was crying on the inside. I would walk out of school with the principal watching me. When he asked me why I left, I looked him straight in the eye and said, "Because I felt like it!" He would give me detention. I earned more detentions in my high school than all the other boys and girls combined.

I did not mind the detention. It caused me to miss the bus, and I would walk the three miles home. It was better to be in detention or walking home by myself than to be surround by the pain and loss in my home.

I found comfort in the butternut tree with my dog at my side. I found relief by writing down my thoughts and feelings. I was proud that I earned good grades. I felt good because I was the only one to continue in school. My sister and brother had both dropped out. I was the only one in my family who graduated from high school and attended college. Nothing I accomplished could gain my mother's acceptance, but I kept trying to make her proud. I carried a smug determination that said, "I'm going to show you that I am a worthwhile person." That determination probably saved my life and my sanity.

I worked hard to feel good about my life, but the grief overwhelmed anything I managed to achieve. The silent cries went on for many years before I got help.

The Butternut Tree

After my brother died, my parents were broken into a million pieces. My other brother got involved in activities that classified him as a juvenile delinquent. My sister got married at seventeen and moved away from home. I felt alone in the world. There was no one I could turn to and no one I could trust. There was no one to talk to. There was no one to comfort me when I had lost so much. I did not understand so many things. What had happened to our family? It was so fractured that the pieces were scattered in the winds of a hundred places. It reminded me of the nursery rhyme: "All the king's horses and all the king's men couldn't put Humpty together again."

My father worked in the city during the week. My mother and I were home alone on the farm. She wasn't much help to me because of the depth of her grief. When she wasn't too depressed to move or talk, she was bragging about the virtues of her beloved dead son. She would talk about what a terrible child my living brother was and how much pain he caused her. It really hurt me when she spoke so uncaringly about my other brother.

To get away from the torment of her soul, I would walk to the end of our property line. There was a wild rice lake, and at the edge of the lake, there was a huge butternut tree. I would climb to the top of the butternut tree and sit there for hours. I could see for miles around me. The view was beautiful.

Our family dog waited for me at the bottom of the butternut tree. He seemed to know that I needed the time and space to heal my wounds. I felt as if he understood my need for love and touch more than any other creature on the earth. He was always at my side with a paw in my lap or a kiss on the cheek. Sometimes he would whimper softly to communicate his feelings to me. He seemed to be saying, "I'm sorry you're so sad. I wish I could help you. You're not alone. I'm here to touch and to hold and to pet." He helped me survive some very difficult years between the ages of eight and eighteen.

The butternut tree and the surrounding countryside had a calming effect on my wounded spirit. I enjoyed watching the woodland creatures as they scampered about in their daily routines. The sunsets were beautiful and painted soft colors in my life, which seemed to be primarily painted black.

The moon would shine brightly enough to light my way back home. The darkness became my friend when my brother was dying. I felt calm and comfort in the dark. The harsh reality of daylight and the tension that came with it frightened me.

The butternut tree held magic for me in those difficult days. In the winter, I would ski back to my butternut tree, climb up to a branch, and think about my life. I would ski for a while, and then my dog and I would ski home. In the summer, I went to my tree in the rain or sunshine. When there were thunderstorm warnings, I still went to my tree. That was not a safe thing to do, but the storms in my life were more threatening than the thunderstorms.

After my brother died, I believed our family would be all right again. Even though I did not accept that the person in the coffin was my brother, I knew my parents believed it. I hoped we would live a happy life after they buried him. That never happened. The family had been so fractured by grief that it could never be fixed.

I remained on the outside, just as my nightmares had warned. I sat with my mother on the night she died. Even though she was in a coma, I waited eagerly for her to awaken and tell me she loved me and was proud of me. She died while I was waiting to hear those lifesaving words. Once she was dead, there was no one left to validate my life. I was fifty-one years old. I had waited since my conception to be loved and accepted. I finally had to accept that the only person who could validate my life was me.

We spend our lives trying to be good enough to be loved by our parents and significant others. We convince ourselves that we are not worthy of love if our own parents cannot love us. What a tragedy!

The Night Monster

Nightmares Following My Brother's Death

The night monster made his first appearance six months after my brother died. I hated falling asleep. I never knew when the night monster would slip into my dreams, but it frightened me to think of it.

The night monster became a regular visitor. That thief in the night robbed me of the sleep I desperately needed to prepare for the next day. This night monster told me that life was not going to improve, and it was going to get worse. It did not seem possible that it could get any worse. Later I soon realized that the night monster was right, and his warnings were accurate.

The nightmares frightened and perplexed me. The scene was always the same. I was standing outside in deep, cold snow. The doors and windows were locked. I was cold and shivering in my wet clothes. I was hungry and exhausted. I had been standing there for longer than I could remember. I wasn't sure if it was days, weeks, or years.

All the lights were on in the house, and everyone

was home. They were all talking to each other and playing a board game. They were all sipping on hot cocoa. I pounded on the door! No one noticed. No one even turned in the direction of the noise. I stared in the windows, pounded on them, and begged them to let me in. No one responded. I started to cry, but I stopped before anyone could see me. I was so cold and hungry. I felt so alone.

I could not understand why they had not noticed that I was missing. I had been gone a long time, and they were carrying on as if I did not exist. Why did not they realize I was missing? How could my mother just forget me? How could they not hear me? I was hurt, confused, and frightened.

When I woke up, the despair was overwhelming. I could not get in, and I could not understand why they did not miss me. I would wake up cold and alone and shivering. The nightmare seemed too real to be a dream. It would take me a long time to get back to sleep.

It would be many years before I realized the significance of that night monster. I had always been on the outside of that family. I had always been alone. The only difference was that all the doors and windows were locked after my brother's death.

(Optional Chapter)
The Hippocratic Oath

Obligation of Medical Doctors—
Truth versus Reality

This book would not be complete without discussing the role of medical and psychiatric doctors and their obligation to their patients relative to the Hippocratic oath. A doctor's failure to commit to this very important oath has caused the death of many patients.

In 2016, the number of deaths caused by the failure to protect patient lives is frightening. Most doctors are not held responsible for the deaths of their patients because of the failure of these doctors.

I read an article recently about a forty-six-year-old doctor who was convicted for the deaths of three of her patients. They died from drug overdoses. Patients traveled long distances to get their drugs because they were easy to get. Between 2007 and 2010, the doctor's office made $5 million for the drugs.

I have been aware of this abuse since I was eleven. Five members of my immediate family died as the result of powerful drugs that were given to them by their doctors. The drugs were mood stabilizers, painkillers, sleep medications, muscle relaxants, tranquilizers, and many more. Two people intentionally overdosed because they wanted to die. They had been abusing drugs for years and never got the help they needed. In some cases, more than one doctor was giving them drugs. Neither doctor knew about the other doctor's treatments.

My sister-in-law's doctor gave her thirty diet pills without knowing anything about her. My mother overdosed many times over the years. My brother slashed his wrists and shot himself in the head. He left a note on his bathroom sink that said, "No one cared." He survived that attempt, but his doctors gave him the drugs he overdosed on a short while later.

I am angry that we have done nothing for people who need help instead of drugs. Perhaps if we make the doctors legally and financially responsible, there will be fewer deaths. The problem is complicated by the death of needy people. When a person overdoses, the family members feel responsible. We do not need more guilt. We need more answers.

In families such as mine the grief has been handed down for centuries. The damage is profound.

About the Author

C. K. Vetsch is the published author of a daily devotional. She has been a certified chemical dependency counselor, a specialist with the elderly, an emergency chaplain, and a nighttime street-crisis counselor. She was also a licensed foster parent for victims of incest and sexual abuse. The author was a "failed abortion," and her parents reminded her that she "didn't have the courtesy to die." She survived out of sheer determination.

Printed in the United States
By Bookmasters